CHARLIE HAIRSTON

Play Your own Cards

The EXTRAORDINARY Inspirational Story of CATHLEEN SWENSON

TRILOGY
A WHOLLY OWNED SUBSIDIARY OF **TBN**

PROFESSIONAL PUBLISHING MEETS POWERFUL PROMOTION

Trilogy Christian Publishers
A Wholly Owned Subsidiary of Trinity Broadcasting Network
2442 Michelle Drive
Tustin, CA 92780
Copyright © 2024 by Charlie Hairston

For information, address Trilogy Christian Publishing
Rights Department, 2442 Michelle Drive, Tustin, CA 92780.
Trilogy Christian Publishing/ TBN and colophon are trademarks of Trinity Broadcasting Network.
For information about special discounts for bulk purchases, please contact Trilogy Christian Publishing.

Trilogy Disclaimer: The views and content expressed in this book are those of the author and may not necessarily reflect the views and doctrine of Trilogy Christian Publishing or the Trinity Broadcasting Network.

10 9 8 7 6 5 4 3 2 1
Library of Congress Cataloging-in-Publication Data is available.
ISBN 979-8-89333-235-3
ISBN 979-8-89333-236-0

Dedicated to Cathy
And her Memory!

AND Dedicated to all the
Cancer Survivors and
Those Spinal Challenged
All over the world.

Acknowledgements

Special Love and
Thank you to all of my Friends,
Supporters, and especially to
My Dear Loved Ones on Both
Sides of the Family.

With out your Encouragement
This Recording and Documentation of
Cathleen's Extraordinary Life would
have never been written or
published for all to see!
I Love You Everyone!

Table of Contents

CHAPTER ONE:

Where Am I?

Cathleen Swenson was born by the grace of God in West Covina, California, on April Fool's Day in 1961. But she was never anybody's fool. People who knew Cathy growing up recall her as a very determined young girl. She loved every moment growing up with her family. That determination would become even more critical when she was a teenager. Cathleen was diagnosed with astrocytoma, which is a brutal cancer of the spine near the skull. From then on, nothing would be the same for her or her family. But then again, maybe that's the way it's supposed to be. Never the same.

Cathleen was like many California kids who grew up in this sunny and hazy paradise. It was post-World War II America, where the economic opportunities for many, though not all, were expanding unless you might be Mexican or Black. But possibilities for the future seemed to blossom and fill the California skyline like the Santa Anna winds, even if the smog was choking off your view of the mountains…and of your life.

As it is today, California in the sixties was a heady and sometimes hedonistic place. There were and are many families shaping the culture of California. But there are also movie stars and television stars, rock stars, surfers and hippies, and that mythical television family, *The Brady Bunch*. Yes, that TV show. These progressive values, which are really just hippie values with tie-dyed shirts and bell-bottom pants, somewhat mirrored the beautiful colors of the freedom and civil rights movement but certainly not the hippie movement by itself. Not Woke, but definitely modern. Could there be a more California family than the Brady Bunch? Maybe, just maybe.... But I might be biased...I give you the wonderful Swenson family!

Against this California backdrop, Cathy grew up with this wonderful and generous family, which included her parents, Pete and Mary, sister Maureen, and brothers, Randy and Steven, who even look like a chip off the old block of Pete. They were there for her through all her adolescent health problems and the later divorcing of her parents. But this story is bigger than that. The family would always provide infinite emotional and loving support for her throughout the trials that she and her entire family would face while mirroring all the changes that our country went through during the last sixty years. But who says life is perfect, anyway? Life's a gift, not a guarantee, no matter which group or identity or subculture you come from— even when you live in California Paradise. And watch out for the forest fires.

Nevertheless, the Colorado River and Balboa Beach were open for business and there were lives to be lived. The family had made many trips to the river, as they called it, with little or no problems for our beautiful and strong Cathy in hiking around it, water skiing it, or camping next to these beautiful waters. This proud river today still struggles to find enough fresh water to feed the five hyper-growing economies of the five states surrounding it.

Hers was a modern California story; her mom and dad had relocated like so many others from elsewhere, in their case the Midwest—Michigan for Mary and South Dakota for Pete. And Michigan is where this story starts because that is where these two would meet before quickly deciding to get married and go west, just like many people had done for centuries, including gold rushes and Indian land giveaways. These newlyweds did not set off to find gold, just a new life for themselves—a life bathed in gold—that is, California golden sunshine!

Cathy's best friend growing up was definitely Linda, who would remain a lifelong friend. They shared secrets that both of them will take to the grave. Linda had come into the picture by way of her parents, who had befriended Pete and Mary in the greater southern California community.

These families would get together or see each other in social groups that the Swenson's are still members of today.

The Fredericksons were another one of these "in like

Flint families." They, too, were a transplanted midwestern family, and lived right across the corner lot from the Swensons on Eddington Drive. They would provide never-ending love, support, friendship and, yes, even entertainment for our dear family for the rest of their lives. You'll see Linda sitting astride one of her lovely horses while allowing her best friend, our Cathy, still walking in her early teens, to pull her around while both were posing during this glorious moment locked in time.

Cathleen said that Steve and Randy always ogled Linda and adored her—they really liked her! Who knows? But we always did later call her "Lovely Linda!"

Linda and Cathy spent countless hours in each other's rooms, talking about boys and other girls, and listening to the deep as religious music coming throughout the seventies. Whether this music was made in London, San Francisco, or right there in Los Angeles, it was and is music that inspired the baby boomers and Gen X and legions thereafter. It challenged the politics of war and peace and inequity and taught you things about sex, drugs, and rock and roll that maybe, just maybe, you should not know when you are a young girl. But all this would go into developing Cathy's determination and curiosity to explore the world, and to play and *live* in the world, whether or not she was later considered "handicapped," "wheelchair bound," "challenged," or "disabled." She would later show that she was oftentimes more able-bodied than many people who had two good legs. But of course, it's not the obstacles that count, it's the HEART through faith that overcomes those obstacles. Being a victim is not fun for anyone; being a victor is where it's at! Cathy was and is an example of THAT kind of heart. She's a victor that we all can learn from and you'll see why.

CHAPTER TWO

Here We Go . . .

Back then, Pete was forever the apple of Cathleen's eye. He was now supporting, as an X-ray technician in prisons and hospitals, a wife and these four children in paradise—in between boating, camping, and mealing (is that a verb?) at local restaurants, such as In and Out Burger, Big Boy, and Vince's Spaghetti. And all of this while at the beck and call of a beeper in a time long before most beepers (much less smartphones) were common. It is rumored Pete still had his beeper until the day he hung up his protective X-ray tech lead vest for good. He went from technologically advanced to technologically obsolete, all with a warm, confident smile on his broad and handsome Scandinavian face.

She had always dearly loved her mom and her dad, but that special father-daughter relationship grew first, especially once she became ensnared in her medical condition. Her life changed slowly at first and then dramatically in her early teen years, just as she was going into the ever-changing world of puberty and deeper self-discovery. One minute she would be running around like kids will always do, and then she would just fall down unexpectedly, even if there was nothing evidently tripping her up.

This happened more and more, with her legs failing often and as a result, Cathy had to spend more and more time in bed with excruciating pain. The pain was so severe that it would cause her to cry out in the day and in the middle of the night. Pete would come upstairs after work to check on her, offering up steely encouragement or gentle compassion, but no one knew what was happening to his baby girl.

Pete, being the proud and well-trained technician, became more like a doctor in thought and analysis, methodically trying to find answers for his middle child and her physical and mental well-being. This doctoral quality of Pete's continued throughout Cathleen's life, as she would always need to run the latest medical diagnosis past her dad…the big-hearted X-ray tech who thinks he's a doctor! Her condition seemed to bring out the softer side of Pete over the long run, and I am sure he would have responded exactly the same way if it had happened to any of his other three children.

The doctors ordered CAT scans (there were no MRIs yet) and eventually were able to identify the cause of this extreme debilitating pain with the off and on paralysis of her lower body. She had astrocytoma, a cancer that develops on the spine, usually just below the head region. This astrocytoma diagnosis came after much analysis and many exploratory surgeries. Young Cathy had many hospital stays while the rest of the family kept living, working, playing, and going to school. The world kept turning and turning outside of her various hospital windows where she would gaze out, wondering what could be next for her.

Cathy did have her mom, Mary, come see her, though not as often as either of them would have liked. As Cathleen was craving the normalcy of home, Mary was nobly keeping things going at home, but she was also dealing with her own problems and growing pains from marrying and having children at such an early age. It was difficult and sometimes unbearable for Cathy's siblings to visit. This was particularly true with Randy, the youngest, who once came to see Cathy, only to burst into tears after entering the hospital room and then abruptly turning around and leaving. Maybe another day. Cathy was oftentimes loaded with pain medication and almost motionless, since any movement would cause extreme pain. That is, if she even could manage to move anything below the chest.

With surgery after surgery, the doctors eventually succeeded in removing the cancer. Job one done. Yet the doctors were left with the decision of whether to risk one more gallant surgery to try and restore Cathleen's full use of her legs. Could they hope to repair the spine, returning all of her feelings in full force?

They tried. But no go. The surgery was a total disaster.

After this final surgical attempt to fix the partial paralysis, she was left with total paralysis below the chest. The doctors had tried to clean and repair the area, but instead it caused more paralysis—a lot more paralysis, and permanent. She could still move her arms and her hands and her neck, thank God. In fact, she still had full use of them but just not anything that moved below there. Nothing. All she was left with below was blood flow and the occasional slight sensation of warmth or coldness, or a dull aching pain. The doctors had tried their best; no one was at fault, no one blamed them, not even Pete, not even God. It just was what it was.

Still, the girl who came into the hospital did get to leave the hospital. Not all of us get to do that. Some of us, maybe most of us eventually, leave the hospital permanently through the back door and into the morgue. However, Cathleen was leaving the hospital *alive*. But the price she had to pay was that now she saw the world from the viewpoint of a new wheelchair. She rolled herself out of the hospital and into the bright California sunshine, her eyes squinting into the bright glare, and into her new life, with cold steel, metal, and rubber as her constant companions.

CHAPTER THREE:

Her New Legs

Now Cathleen would have to get used to looking down at legs that did not work but would have to be brought along for the ride. She knew she had to keep going; she just didn't know how. But she had her faith in God, faith that had been shared with her at the local California Baptist church, which was a little different from the Southern kind. Her mom and dad dropped off the kids at the church for many years, maybe knowing the children might need it someday—maybe more than they did themselves. She had her friends and neighbors, including Linda, and, most importantly, she had her family. With that support, she would learn how to move again, just as countless others have done through the centuries. Probably ever since the wheel was invented, people have been using them to move, even when the body would not cooperate. Hence, the reason Steven, her kindly but strong-willed brother, would affectionately come to call her "wheels."

In order to make life just a little more manageable at home, Pete and the boys built a new bedroom downstairs for Cathleen. When Steven would come home from work or school, he would go into Cathy's new room and turn her body for her. She advised him how to do it just right so she could get comfortable and so that her skin was protected from being damaged by being in the same position too long.

She started going to rehabilitation classes, often accompanied by Mary, to learn how to function, how to live, how to move from point A to Point B, from within and from without a wheelchair, as they were now her new legs and now her lifelong shadow. She was instructed on how to steer and control the wheels carefully. Years later, I came to know just how tricky this could be because she would scold me for accidentally grabbing her wheels without thinking and then putting her in danger of crashing to the ground!

In training (better known as rehab), the therapist showed her how to transfer, as in lifting yourself with your arms to throw or catapult yourself (slightly) out of the wheelchair and onto a regular chair, such as a restaurant booth, a car seat, a bed, a shower chair. She even had to learn how to get herself up off the floor in case she fell. They taught her how to will herself up by pulling her body up without help from anyone, using nothing but the strength of her arms and shoulders. "No matter how long it takes or how hard it is, you have to be able to recover by yourself," the therapist had said. You had to get completely back up high, into the safe confines of "the chair." This agonizing exercise was particularly excruciating for Mary, who practically had tears in her eyes as she watched her courageous daughter attack her new lifestyle with grit and struggle. Nevertheless, these were her new wheels, and they were the key to her independence.

CHAPTER FOUR:

Why Me?

Even though it might be a dark place, we can all get stuck, clinging to our current situation because it is comfortable and familiar, even when a better place is right around the corner with a little more work. If only we will just believe, pray, and never give up! Don't you ever give up!

Pete knew his daughter had to keep going no matter what. More than anyone else, he would encourage her to just keep going, telling her that things have a way of working themselves out. This South Dakota and Scandinavian can-do spirit is Pete's way of living, even though he is not religious, spiritual, or particularly in touch with the Divine. He still believes in the physical world, in reality, in the human spirit to overcome obstacles. He has learned to do that more and more throughout his life, while adding more patience and love in the process. Cathy and her new condition brought out the softer side of him. It changed him to see his dear middle child, his offspring, struggle so mightily but still *fight* on with grace.

But Pete and Mary kept a very dark and scary secret between them that the doctors had shared only with them. It would not be revealed to anyone, particularly Cathleen, until much, much later. The secret was that the doctors believed that Cathy probably would not live to see the dawn of her twenty-fifth birthday. Her body would not hold up; she was on a limited amount of time. But then again, aren't we all?

With the help and support of her family, friends, and community, Cathy started going back to high school. Long before President Bush, the senior, pushed through the Americans with Disabilities Act (ADA)[1], Mr. Warner, one of Steven and Cathleen's favorite teachers, and other caring teachers and administrators, had special ramps built to help her and her wheelchair get up some of the more stubborn steps and difficult terrain that lay about the Upland High School campus.

But high school was still high school. Teasing and bullying have been a fact of life since the beginning of time, and Cathy's situation was no different. Children and adults will tease or be condescending toward each other, but the key is that it never be accompanied with violence or the threat of violence. That threat was NEVER there. But respect for others and other groups is what we strive for and should be the rule of the day. But we are not all going to be nice or love each other all the time. Zero tolerance is an unrealistic idea and a bad method that goes against human nature.

But having a tough and strong brother usually gets the job done, and Cathleen had that in Steven. He quickly let people know not to mess with his big sister and would shoo away anyone, I mean anyone, who would try to bother or ridicule her.

Maureen, on the other hand, was the older sister by a couple of years, and she was wise enough to show Cissy (as Maureen forever called her) the ropes. Maureen loved life like most any American teenager and would go to music concerts such as California Jam and The US Festival, just down the road a piece from their home in southern California. These were huge youth musical gatherings where artists such as Ted Nugent, U2, Van Halen, Deep Purple, and the Clash would cut their teeth in the seventies and eighties. Cathy would pick up the latest in youth culture from her older sister, just like a lot of us did. Even after all she had gone through, life for Cathleen was now becoming fun again. Maureen helped her see this.

Maureen would take Cathy to memorable parties and gatherings where it was rumored very strongly that alcohol was being consumed by high schoolers! Imagine that. But people coming of age have always tried to emulate their parents and those older than themselves. Cathy was no different and always felt like she learned a lot hanging out with her well-balanced, no-nonsense older sister. She never forgot how at one party a reveler had too much to drink and was throwing around beer bottles. Boys will be boys. But one landing a bit too close to Cathy's head was a little scary.

Teenagers need to be protected from themselves because the brain still has not completely developed yet. The last thing we should be doing is asking teenagers to make life-altering decisions in their teen years! It can often work itself out once maturity has had a chance to catch up.

While we are at it, maybe we should decriminalize the passageway to adulthood, while still teaching loads of common sense, with tons of encouragement. Bringing this back to a traditional focus without all the legalities and zero tolerances. This would most definitely have a better chance of producing mature, well-balanced, and hopefully, happy adults, while not setting back so many lives that are just trying to get their feet on the ground. The feet that God gave them while figuring it all out on the way to adulthood and *life*.

CHAPTER FIVE:

I'm Ready to Fly

After a couple of rough up and down years, emotionally and spiritually, for Cathleen and the family, Cathy started to become almost fearless and earnest in almost everything! She put her mind to it all as her high school graduation came and went and young adulthood opened up before her bright and wide blue eyes. This is what she had been waiting for since childhood and, whether she was in a wheelchair or not, she was going to start living life to the fullest and experience whatever the world had waiting for her.

But first, Cathleen had to start driving to get herself around. For this, hand controls were installed on the "Mav" (the family's nickname for their 1971 Ford Maverick), the spare car that most of the Swenson kids drove for a time as a passageway to getting their own wheels. Of course, it could be dangerous, but her parents knew that she needed to experience life and to be independent. No helicopter parents here! And independent was a word we would all hear more and more from Cathy as she *fought* to live her life on her own terms, just as most of us do, except for her it was a step harder. She would not be denied anything and started getting various jobs to save money for her next step up in life. With a little help, she and Pete were able to find a sporty '66 Ford Mustang convertible that she made her own by adding hand controls. She looked like a natural riding around Southern California with the top down, sunglasses on, and a cool expression on her face as she cut through the Santa Anna winds.

By this time, her brothers and sister were graduating, working, and living in and out of the house. Mary and Pete, unfortunately, separated and eventually divorced. Cathleen was now living at home with her dad and an ever-changing combination of her sister and brothers, plus not too much later, some of her four new stepsisters brought into her life after Pete remarried. Cathy's new step mom, Eva, being from Taft, in the central Californian high desert, was ready, willing, and eager to start a new, bountiful life and household with Pete with a fluctuating cast living there with them.

After driving back and forth to try out Chafee Community College for a couple of semesters (not for her!), she settled into a new job commuting the one-hour long traffic filled drive to downtown Los Angeles, where she worked from the early morning hours at a firm there in the middle of the LA skyline until each sunset-filled evening.

Our girl would not be talked out of it nor be denied the adventure and better pay that this downtown LA job offered. "Yes, I'll take care of myself! No, no one is going to mug me or rob me!" she would say. Still, many of her dear friends and family thought she was crazy for working in this inner city not too far from Hollywood (as many would not work in that area at that time or even now).

Many nights, Cathy would come home late and get herself into the house after another exhausting commute back from her budding career downtown, and she would find Randy and Steven flopped out on the sofas relaxing and watching TV. "Get up and do something with your life," she would say to her brothers. The boys protested that they were simply relaxing after working hard at their jobs all day! But Cathleen probably did not hear them, because she was too busy planning what she was going to do tomorrow, the next day and for the rest of her life.

CHAPTER SIX:

I Can Do This

During this time of new horizons, Cathleen traveled to Oahu, Hawaii with Maureen when they were only two or three years removed from high school. Back then people, including young women, were bolder and less afraid to venture out into the world, even though crime was higher at that time. But it was more important to live life than to protect it within a cocoon. If you don't live now, when will you?

But there were some big challenges on this Oahu trip. Their car broke down in the Hawaiian countryside, and with no cell phones in those days, Maureen had to leave Cathy in the car while she hiked down the old dirt road to look for help. When a military man and his girlfriend drove up, Maureen hesitated but decided she had better get in because she did not know where else to go. Everything turned out okay; Maureen was able to get help, and their car was on the way soon. Then, years before disabled rooms and parking spaces, Maureen had to press the travel agency three times to try three different places before they finally had a bathroom that Cathy would be able to get her wheelchair into, otherwise she would have been in a bad predicament. Think about being stuck in a car all day and not being able to stop and go!

They had a good time, but Maureen was still worried that Cissy (as she called her) would not want to travel anymore after all the inconveniences. Not to worry, Cathleen would still catch the traveling bug, taking another trip to Hawaii shortly after that with her best friend Linda and traveling all over the world as much as she could. Lots of fun was to be had, and she was not going to miss out on any of it or the adventure it promised. Maybe most of us, in time, start to take exciting opportunities for granted. But not this amazing spirit! She seemed to treat every opportunity, every possibility, every challenge as a gift from God—which is exactly what it is! She could not afford to take anything for granted. She came to look at all these moments and challenges as grand adventures because they were not easy for her. Even if it was just taking a trip to Hawaii, she faced obstacles that could be overcome and felt the feelings of success that followed. It was a glorious victory for her... and a blessing.

It was around this time that she took up scuba diving, despite everyone in her family thinking she was dangerously crazy. After all, she was now officially a paraplegic and each one of them was worrying about her safety! Wasn't she glad to just be alive? Her brother Steven even called Pete to ask why he was letting her put her life and their sanity in danger. He responded, "Well, she wants to do it and she feels she can do it."

In fact, the scuba diving experience was one of the most satisfying, intense, and bravest things that Cathy ever did in her life. Like the rest of her scuba classmates, this courageous woman would have to bring herself up out of the water from a regular dive off the back of a boat and literally lift herself with her dangling legs up onto dry land. Easier said than done, right? For her dive mates, it was very difficult and scary, what with timing your exit from the ocean by way of the beach with Pacific sized waves crashing all around you while the undertow is pulling you back out. Added to that are weighted air tanks and cumbersome breathing apparatus strapped to your body and face.

For Cathleen, it was daunting and near impossible since her legs could help her neither negotiate the waves nor walk up the slowly rising shoreline towards the beach. With herculean effort, exhausting concentration, and an instructor swimming nearby, this determined and stubborn person was able to eventually start overpowering the crashing waves and relentless undertow. Breathing heavily, her heart racing, she had to prevent herself from turning over every time a large wave crashed over her as she slowly pulled her body towards the shoreline.

Now, things would get even harder. She had to time herself just right to land upright on the shoreline underwater so she would not turn over. Then she crawled using just her hands and elbows while dragging her entire body and floppy legs from the rear, inch by inch, lurch by lurch, yard by yard, making her way agonizingly through the shallow waters up, up, up until she was completely out of the water.

When her legs were finally out of the crashing waves and undertow of the Pacific, she collapsed on top of the moist sand in a heap of raw exhaustion and hot tears, weeping her eyes out. Cathy was physically and mentally spent. But she had made it; she had done it! When asked why she did all of this when the instructor would certainly have let her skip and take a pass on it due to her condition, she said, "I figured if everyone else had to do it, then shouldn't I?" Cathy came within one dive of getting her certification. Been there, done that. She was already off exploring other adventures!

CHAPTER SEVEN:

There Is So Much I Need to Do

Continuing her adventures, Cathleen also went traveling with a couple of girlfriends from work. They went down to Mexico where she learned to say, "Dos cervezas, por favor"—Spanish for two beers, please! Cathy was from the new California where most of her family and friends did not know or even care to understand Spanish, even though California had long been Mexican territory (before being won in the Mexican-American War) and most of the places and things were in Spanish. But that had been "mostly" settled in 1848. I guess that was the point—not anymore!

This was basically the extent of the exercises in Spanish, except for Steven's occasional telling of a totally filthy and dirty joke in Spanish that he had learned from one of his hard-working coworkers...followed by wonderful howls of "Oh, Steven!" It was from this that we learned what Johnny Carson, the late-night television host and icon, meant for all those decades when he would say "caca" while smirking and staring into the camera in front of all of America! (Just look it up.)

But this undeterred modern woman was having loads of fun down in the heart of Mexico, trying to learn some Spanish while hanging out at the sunny pools and resorts with her girlfriends (the term used forever to refer to a woman's platonic female friends…nothing else in this case) and catching the attention of a lot of young men who would all be bedazzled by her sparkling blue eyes and beautiful hazel hair.

But the trip immediately turned scary as Cathleen suddenly fell ill and had to be airlifted to a Caribbean hospital in the Cayman Islands to get the advanced emergency care and treatment that she needed. What to do? As a medical professional, Pete monitored the deteriorating situation closely with her doctors and nurses while stuck at his job and responsibilities in California. But this loving parent quickly arranged to pay and supplement the income of one of the girls on the trip so that this girlfriend would be financially able to stay there with Cathy for weeks and be an advocate for her in this foreign land.

It was said she had some kind of internal infection. The fear and worry went on agonizingly for weeks, keeping family and friends on pins and needles once more. They hoped that this was not what they had feared for years… that one day this could be it.

But this proud paraplegic woman could thank the Lord that it was nowhere near the end. Our hero fought back patiently and quietly in this away-from-home hospital bed with a window view. She bounced back in a few weeks' time, and she triumphantly returned to her life back home in southern California on Eddington Street, telling everyone all about her exciting but scary trip and all her stories of dos cervezas and boys, as if it were just another chapter in a charmed life.

And you know what? It was. In fact, God was about to bless her with a brand-new life-changing career, and it was just around the next bend!

CHAPTER EIGHT

Come Fly with Me!

Not content to just be working at one of her ever-improving jobs during the day, Cathleen was giving back by mentoring disabled girls, teaching kids' wheelchair tennis, and in the evening by helping out on an abused women's hotline. On many nights at the House of Ruth, she would listen, encourage, and advise other women who were facing their own difficulties in life. Although some might pity her because of her wheelchair, she always thought of herself as blessed. Wheelchair or not, she knew she had it good, and she wanted to help others who might be in very desperate situations.

While doing all this, she was also working hard, advancing, and improving her position every time she changed jobs or careers. This enlightened woman was also saving money as quickly as she could while still living at home with Pete and Eva and a wonderful revolving door of brothers and stepsisters. She was making friends and admirers wherever she worked while she was planning and dreaming of that day when she might get a chance to be on her own.

It has always been true that every boy and girl dreams of one day being successful and self-sufficient, and Cathleen was not any different. In fact, maybe even more so. Through one of her girlfriends, Cathy heard about a career path in airline reservations with the now defunct TWA, the mighty Trans World Airlines, which had been the brainchild of the eccentric billionaire Howard Hughes.

This is when the airline industry was starting to expand flights everywhere, lowering ticket prices to make vacationing and flying to other locales more affordable for the average person. Up until this time, flight arrangements had been handled in person at ticket counters and with travel agents. But now it was developing that people would contact the airline directly over the phone more. This era was laughingly called the information age—little did we know that we would be buried by this so-called "information" over the next two decades with the perfection of the PC and the smartphone. As far as what qualified for information, what was that Spanish word that Johnny Carson had used on TV so often? Anyway, she got the job! She started working with TWA Airline Reservations there in good old southern California.

This self-taught businesswoman loved her new career and excelled at it. She drove into work on time every day and was blessed to get along with all her coworkers and managers. Everyone, including Pete, was inspired and impressed with how well Cissy was doing managing her life. This wonderfully determined young woman was making friends and attending all family functions, including weddings, particularly mother Mary's wedding to her devoted boyfriend, Don.

Except for a couple of hiccups, life was going great for all of the family here in this sunny paradise. In fact, the smog and California air were even improving, along with the view of the beautiful San Gabriel Mountains. The visibility of Mount Baldy, the local ski slope, and all of the mountains and valleys around Los Angeles had bounced back to their earlier allure and grandeur after smog controlling legislation had gone into effect. Thank you, sunny California, for becoming beautiful again.

This proud physically challenged woman was now in her mid to late twenties and was continuing to do great things with TWA Reservations. As she moved up and up, she applied for a new job with TWA as a business analyst. Although many of the business analysts in this industry have college degrees, Cathy did not. In fact, she believed she could do it just as well or better without a degree. Maybe that is a good attitude we should follow as a nation as we grapple with soaring college tuition and record-breaking student debt. Many high-paying jobs do not necessarily need the qualification of a degree, and maybe it's time our economy started to reflect that.

But a big step and a *real* career awaited Cathleen.

The challenge, however, was that the job offer was for a business analyst situated at TWA's headquarters or HUB (as they are called in the airline industry) in Kansas City, Missouri—halfway across the North American continent from her home. Nevertheless, she went to the interview, and this determined focused woman wowed the recruiters, and she got the job offer along with a financial package to move across the country.

After accepting the position, she told her dad about her plans to move. One can imagine his initial anguish and fear for this dear middle child who already had so many health problems and was operating from a wheelchair. But at least she had been near her loving family! His reaction was of honest shock and surprise. Pete told her that out of all his children, Cathleen was the last one he expected to be saying goodbye to and helping move across the country. To this day, that fact is still true.

But moving plans were made, and packing was done. Cathy said goodbyes to her mom, who was settling in quite nicely in her new life with Don, and to her sister Mo (as Maureen is affectionately known), and to everyone else. In fact, Cathleen said goodbye to all of her girlfriends, who had already been through so much with her, particularly Linda, who was getting married and moving in a new direction in her own life. Everyone was exploring new life and horizons were opening up.

Pete and the boys packed up her Mustang and the

moving truck that he had rented for her small belongings and little furniture. Cissy said her goodbyes, and she pulled out of Upland, California with Pete and the truck right behind her. Cutting across the lower desert and the foothills of the Rockies and into the state of New Mexico, Cathleen, with her wheelchair next to her, headed towards a new life that was going to be on her own terms in the Midwest land of Missouri. And she was going to SHOW them a thing or two...Bam.

CHAPTER NINE

Kansas City, Here I Come!

Cathleen traveled safely across the country in her hand-controlled Mustang, after only a few days reaching Kansas and then across the line into Kansas City, Missouri. Then they slowly unpacked her things for her new life. Pete helped her set up and figure out how she would operate and get around in her new place. Almost too quickly, it seemed, it was time for Pete to go back. Life and work were calling him as well. So, Pete and Cathy turned in the rental truck, said their goodbyes and I-love-yous, and the loyal daughter drove the loving father to the airport, where she watched his plane take off as Pete returned to the safety of her original home and family in California.

But now this enlightened girl had a new home and Cathy embraced this new adventure that she was on. "You only live once, so you better make the most of it now!" she would say. Cathleen soon met Ruthie, her dear neighbor, in a nearby unit in this apartment complex. She would become another one of Cathy's lifelong friends, and is still loyal to her to this day.

Cathleen had decided beforehand that it was time that she lived alone; that she would do things her own way. We would *all* see a lot more of that from her in the future! Anyway, a lot of single women to this day, a lot of people with two good legs, would think it not a good idea or even scary to live in an apartment by themselves—but not this bold, courageous person! She had no roommates, and at first, very few connections outside of her work, and all in a strange new city and region. Plus, Cathleen had an apartment and a bathroom that were definitely *not* made for a wheelchair.

She did, however, have a covered parking spot for her car. Still, after parking during the winter, she would then have to trudge through the snow and ice with her hands freezing from all the muck on her wheels, to get into her ground level apartment (which again was not handicap accessible). This was all usually by herself before and after work, either in the early morning or later in the evening. In fact, the snow and ice had often built up on and around the sidewalks throughout the freezing winters. Sometimes she thought "Why me?" but not often. She was just glad to be *alive*.

Her new apartment bathroom was another great challenge that she had to overcome. The bathroom was not up to ADA standards, with the standards being only for new buildings being built or else grandfathered in only when there was a remodeling, so Cathy's narrow bathroom was still very narrow. In fact, this woman in a wheelchair would have to slide and transfer her body onto a dining room chair that Pete or Ruthie had strategically placed in the bathroom for her. Then each time, Cathleen would have to thrust her body over and over again to get the chair to even slide on the floor, inch by inch, closer and slowly closer, as it moved toward the toilet seat or the bathtub. Then, Cathy would have to use all of her strength and arms to get onto the toilet or into the bathtub and out again, eventually to do what she needed to do…every time…every day…every week…for YEARS and years of determined effort.

Nevertheless, she made it work and stayed there for many winters and several years. Something that we all take for granted was something that Cathleen Swenson and millions of other people have had to figure out! God bless the human spirit to keep adapting and changing!

CHAPTER TEN:

Home on My Terms

Our role model of inspiration and determination threw herself into her new work but also dove into creating a normal, respectable home—a place she could be proud of, even one so modest. She made friends and explored the city when she wasn't working her long hours. The downtown entertainment district was where everyone went. They followed the professional sports teams, mostly the Kansas City Royals baseball team, but Cathy's favorite to follow was definitely the Kansas City Chiefs football team. Cathleen would continue to follow the Chiefs long after she had moved out of the state. She was still pulling for them for the rest of her life from then on, right up through the Chiefs winning their second championship in five years with their awesome quarterback, Patrick Mahomes!

With wonderful friends like Ruthie nearby, Cathy always sought ways to work around and overcome any challenge that stood in her way and to always have fun. We all need family and friends and close neighbors and real communities, not just imagined communities on social media, which are okay for grouping and broadcasting, hopefully, *positive* information and entertainment. But for thousands of years, humankind has needed real friends in the physical world. It does take a real village, a real neighborhood. No one…no one succeeds alone, not even Cathy—not anyone.

CHAPTER ELEVEN:

Analyze THIS!

This grown girl worked hard to fit in and learned to become a business analyst in travel. Again, Cathy succeeded without a college degree, even though it is often required or expected. But she knew she could do this too. A brighter day still lay ahead, and she *believed* in this. She truly believed that God would never give someone more than they could handle—not even her.

Cathy adopted a cat for her apartment and named her Bailey. Bailey was standoffish and would stay under the bed or sofa for hours upon hours or even for half the day, coming out to eat only to go right back into hiding. Imagine that! Even though they were not really that close, she and Bailey had each other, and that was what counted, I guess.

Maybe once or twice a year, particularly at the holidays, she would go back to California, since this was the time when employees in the airline industry (and sometimes their families) could fly for free.

When the family came from California to see her, it

was a very special event in her life. When her mom and Mo or her dad and Eva and Steve, even Randy, would be able to come, she would take pictures with everyone holding the cat. There was also always a *long* list of favors to ask: "Could you please move this?" "Could you help me get that down…no, *that*…" "Would you please rehang this picture over there?" "Dad, could we repair or fix this? Steve?" Everyone was so proud of her and the life that she was building on her own, despite being in a wheelchair and a thousand miles away from the family.

The family was always patiently and eagerly ready to help Cathy, they always had been. It does take a community, and it almost always takes a loving family. Have compassion for those who do not have a strong family structure and maybe encourage them to build a strong family value system for their next generation. There was a *lot* of love there between all of them for their Cath. I think she inspired them with her grace and determination and touched everyone's hearts forever.

After several years in Kansas City, the airline reservation system she worked under which served TWA, Delta, and Northwest Airlines, was merged into one and spun off into a new corporation called World Span. This new entity would relocate to the home of Delta Airlines, one of the largest and fastest growing airlines in the country, and to the busiest airport in the country.

Cathleen and her department were immediately

transferred to Atlanta, Georgia, where she would continue her adventures, buying a house and pursuing *all* of her dreams.

CHAPTER TWELVE:

The City Of...Atlanta!

Atlanta was, and still is, the home of the Civil Rights movement in the USA, largely due to it being the home of the Nobel Peace prize winning leader, Dr. Martin Luther King, Jr. It is also because of its headquarters for the Coca-Cola company and its famous chairman, Robert W. Woodruff, showing calm and leadership when other cities were rioting or burning and declaring that Atlanta was the city "too busy to hate."

It was also the one city in the Southern States during the American Civil War that absolutely had to be captured, no matter what. Located in the foothills of the southeastern corner of the country, it had recently become a huge transportation hub in the new growing railroad industry, which had only developed during the decades just before the war.

After it was captured, subdued, and mostly burned to the ground, the groundwork had been laid for the conclusion of the devastation of the American Civil War. A war that ended slavery in the Americas and ushered in the emerging industrial revolution. By far, it cost more lives and property loss than all the other wars in American history combined. In time, this magnificent city would rise again into a very modern city.

In fact, when Cathleen was moving to Atlanta, it had become so modern compared to its past that it had been chosen to host the worldwide Summer Olympic Games. Civic pride was on hyper-steroids! After dizzying growth and expansion for many decades, now the city would take great pride in celebrating its place on the world stage. This is the environment that Cathy found herself in as she moved to this growing metropolis, and it was mostly a blast!

When the Olympics and the world finally arrived in Atlanta in 1996, Cathy proudly volunteered to help with the Paralympic Games and Festivities, which were always held in the same year and often in the same city as the traditional Olympics. She took great pride in all that she had overcome in her life and definitely held an affinity with all challenged people, particularly the world-class athletes who were pushing and pursuing their dreams at such a high level.

This proud paralyzed woman wanted to celebrate all athletes who gave it all they had, even those with physical (or sometimes mental) challenges of their own. She even kept her Paralympic volunteer cap and uniform just to remind herself of this special summer in her life. It was a great time for her and the whole city.

Atlanta was now an international city, for better or for worse. A decade later in the early 2000s, the city, with the advantages of its history and geographic location (and after obscene tax breaks were offered), would become a major film and television hub, producing just under the amount that Southern California does from whence she came. Maybe she was the secret weapon.

CHAPTER THIRTEEN

Takin' the Red-Eye

Just a couple of years before this, the internet and the world wide web were created by Congress and were being developed as a military information system to help bring about an end to the Cold War with the Soviet Union. As the USSR fell and our western priorities changed to peaceful ideas and communication, we in the West started opening up the internet and world wide web to being used for more private and social functions. Change came slowly, but deliberately, ultimately coming on like a tsunami, connecting all the personal computers of the world with messaging and even visuals. The sky was the limit! Little did we know where it would all lead.

The airline industry was one of the first to find a practical use for this new technology, which was perfect for the needs of their reservation systems. Cathleen's job was on the cusp of this exciting new wave of technology. Her work would require her to travel all around the world, usually all by her lonesome little self. She wound up in places like London, Paris, Tokyo, Cape Town, South

Africa, and Hamburg, Germany, where her company had a huge office.

She took red-eye (overnight) trips to these capitals and big cities of Europe. She traveled by herself with just a duffel bag of clothes in her lap as she wheeled and propelled herself and her wheelchair proudly through countless airports in America and Europe. People would turn their heads and look at her sometimes, but she did not care, she loved it! She confidently went through security alone, hailed cabs, rented cars with hand controls, checked into hotels, and navigated the shuttles and buses that hopefully were wheelchair accessible. Though she did this all by herself, she still welcomed whatever help and kindness from people that she could find. None of us truly do anything alone. We each have angels and caregivers all around us, helping us through life. But it starts with yourself. It started with Cathy and her willingness to believe in herself.

She would often sleep alone, sprawled out on some red-eye flight (money was flush then and the airlines often had many empty seats), getting just a few hours of this fitful sleep while lying across several seats by lifting the armrests. Once landed, she would rush off to a strategy meeting being held that same morning in some far away office building in the middle of that European city, wherever her company needed her. She was never scared or worried that she was alone. Yes, she was smart and cautious, but determined, and she was *living* the best she could! No one was going to mess with her—and they never did! She *loved* it and she met so many wonderful dear friends that she always counted to the end. What a blessed life.

Two of these dear friends are Mary and Carey. They were chums and sisters from the beginning. All three of them together were single, proud gals and rising businesswomen in an airline industry that was, at that point, still dominated by men but changing fast. Sometimes they all worked for the same company and boss, other times for direct competitors, and still other times working somewhere in the airline and travel industry, but always close by.

Carey and Mary and other gals in the industry would gather after work or on weekends, or go on pleasure trips together around the world. Cathy worked hard, and she played hard along with her girlfriends. Some of their other friends would be from the European offices, some from the other American offices. Somehow, when a layover would occur, the parties would begin! Dos cervezas, por favor?

Cathy was becoming worldly! The girl from California, instead of waiting for the whole world to come to her, was evermore going further out into the world, finding new friends from Kansas City, Atlanta, and New York, as well as England, Ireland, France, and India just to name a few.

Among these many, many other friends were Jeremy and his wife, Lisa; their dear friend Simon; and Jeremy's sister, Diana (just like the princess!). Being British (except for Lisa, who is American), they were all working together in the ever-expanding world of travel. Jeremy and Cathleen ended up becoming dear best friends throughout the nineties and beyond. He brought Cathy a Eurocentric and world-wise view into her life, and when in Atlanta or across the pond, was always able to lift her spirits in friendship.

Once on a trip back to California, Jeremy and Simon and some of the others followed Cath to come stay with her at her mother Mary's house, the house that Cathy had grown up in. Cathy could not have been prouder of all that she and her family had overcome and accomplished. How fantastic that Jeremy and the guys got along with Mary and Cathleen's stepfather, Don, as well as Steven, who was living there with his mom.

CHAPTER FOURTEEN:

"Flyin' the Sonic Boom"

The dot-com boom of the nineties, marked by the rapid growth of the internet and the world wide web (as it was known at the time), was a transformative period. It was reshaping not only Cathy's life but also the lives of everyone, including the broader impact on our country's economy. It was destined to revolutionize how we all engage with technology, bringing the good with the not so good!

Jeremy and his best friend, Simon, were constantly meeting up with Cath, flying somewhere together or working together in Atlanta. It was a great time in her life. In fact, rumor has it that Jeremy and Lisa fell for each other in a new and special way, right there at a small party at Cathy's house. Jeremy and Lisa wound up moving to the South of France together (still working for one of the internet reservation companies) and made plans to get married and start a family together there.

In the near future, Cathy packed her duffel bag once more and set off for Valbonne on the French Riviera. Her mission? To witness Jeremy and Lisa's beautiful wedding in the charming village chapel that had stood since the Middle Ages, dating back to around 1100 AD. Life was indeed fun for our hero.

Following the wedding ceremony and as the festivities wound down, Linda, Cathy's best friend from California, joined her along with Mary and Carey, who had also journeyed to Valbonne for the wedding. The four friends rented a van and skillfully helped Cathy and her wheelchair into the spacious back storage area, embarking on an adventure together.

They drove out of Valbonne and onto the coastal highway, heading straight down the French coast. Every few hours, they stopped to explore the beautiful shoreline and architecture that dates all the way back to the Roman Empire. They drove through hairpin turns along the narrow highway as it changed from the French Alps to the Italian Alps. Cathy and the gals found quaint and enchanting coffee shops and hotels along with breathtaking views of the Mediterranean Sea, often on cliffs a hundred feet above the water. "Keep blowing the horn as we go around the hairpin turns," the girls reminded each other, "or we could blow it altogether!"

The city of Siena, in Tuscany, with its carved out chapels and narrow winding streets, might have been the prettiest destination. Or was it Santa Margarita or Portofino, with its stunning but tiny mountainside harbor where fisherman and sidewalk artists have gathered and sold their wares for centuries? Who knows which of the places was the best? That's just Italy, with its perfection everywhere. It was all part of the trip of a lifetime; one that Cathy would never stop remembering with her girls.

On another one of her trips back to California for the holidays, Cathy's very young nephew, Trevor, would share with her how he realized that his aunt Cissy was different. This wheelchair…what was that? I'm a big boy and Aunt Cissy should be walking just like me. Being so young, he thought it was from lack of trying. He knew that if he had mastered the skill of walking, his aunt could too! He just knew it, and has always been mentally strong all the way through adulthood, becoming an attorney. So, the very young Trevor gathered himself one day and rushed up to his dear Aunt Cissy, saying, "Come on, Aunt Cissy, just try, you can do it. You can learn to walk just like me. Just try!" After the laughter subsided, Cathy realized that Trevor, of course, did not know that his aunt's spine had been severed by the doctors to help her get around in the wheelchair and that her hamstrings had been disconnected as well so that her feet would not point upward while sitting. It was now impossible for her to walk again.

About this time, the unthinkable happened again. Cathy started to feel worn down and sick. Many days she could barely get through work and had to give it everything she had to just make it through the day. She did not know what was going on, but she knew it was not good. Living by herself there in her Atlanta house, she was barely able to take care of herself while in this condition.

Atlanta does have the best, if not one of the greatest, spinal hospitals in the world. The Shepherd Spinal Center, founded by the Shepherd family in response to their own son's debilitating spinal condition, is one of the best in the world for aiding individuals and their families in adapting to life in a wheelchair or dealing with spinal injuries, regardless of whether they resulted from an accident or a birth defect. This hospital is equipped with a state-of-the-art rehabilitation center, a gym, an indoor swimming pool, and hundreds of beds for patients and their families. It is similar to St. Jude Children's Research Hospital in Memphis.

Many people from the whole country, if they are the lucky ones, come here for treatment and training and lifestyle adjustments after the discovery of a mobility-threatening illness or a spine-changing car or work accident. I guess it is good that they are there for all of us, in case we need it one day!

Cathy connected with the Shepherd Center after coming to Atlanta. She had many of her numerous medical checkups and follow-ups there. Many people who are living and constantly maneuvering in a wheelchair must watch out for skin issues due to the great amount of stress and friction that occurs while living in a wheelchair. Bladder and kidney stones also occur regularly and are much more common for a person living in a wheelchair. Cathy had bladder stone issues for years and had to have them laser-zapped or outright surgically removed many, many times.

If you are a girl or a woman, you also have extra issues dealing with UTIs or urinary tract infections, which are often caused by the body, mostly in the sitting position all day, being contorted in a way that it was not normally meant to be. This became Cathy's norm, but it still was not the normal standard position of the human body and thus there were lots of issues. She constantly had to watch out for this and periodically take antibiotics to rid her body of the spread of infection, and she stayed focused on it with true Cathy determination!

Cathy also enrolled in and connected with the wheelchair basketball league there at the gym inside Shephard Center. She would show up often and play in a fun, competitive tournament or just show up for pick-me-up games around the court. She met many other inspiring people in similar circumstances this way. Some were dealing with it way better than others.

There was a lot of depression within the community, obviously and understandably. Some of the guys and gals were spiritually and mentally lifting themselves up to new and better heights, allowing the challenge of the wheelchair as a springboard to new awareness and new gifts that otherwise might have never been found. Others were maintaining well and getting by—trying hard and with lots of help to live and maintain a good lifestyle. Of course, there is some overlapping of those two lifestyles, but one attitude might be even more powerful than the other when coupled with tremendous *faith* in something; the *best* being with God, no matter what the religion. This is always the highest power to tap into because it releases eternal purpose, life-creating energy, and the highest form of love known to humankind, that is, God-like love that we can only imagine because it is *so* perfect and forgiving in every way and every circumstance imaginable to the human mind.

But still many others she met were in the dumps, bitter, lost or caught up in their regret or their pain, and still not coming to terms with where they were at this very moment. But I guess that is the way life is across the board. Some of us are reaching for new heights, no matter what obstacles lay before us, which is part of God's plan, while others are working hard just to get by, even wonderfully. Many of us ask, "Why me? What is happening to me?" and can be overwhelmed by fear and anxiety and always feeling persecuted about the future.

But we all have obstacles and fearfulness and worries. It's the counterbalancing of faith and belief that we all must *seek* to balance that fear out with. That is, find the true vibe; find it in God; find it positively in your chosen religion, whichever that may be. And Cathy's chosen way was faith in God through Jesus because faith in Jesus also adds in not just the perfect love of "God" but also the perfect forgiveness and infinite salvation of Jesus.

But however you understand God and the Higher Power, worship it, and find positive belief like Cathy did. Balance out the fear and, in fact, overwhelm your fear with positivity, faith, and power. Cathy and her unbreakable faith and attitude and strong willpower were definitely in that first group!

In her everyday life, Cathy also took up wheelchair tennis and joined one of the many great tennis leagues throughout metro Atlanta, which has more amateur tennis leagues of all kinds than anywhere else in the world! You would think it was still the seventies and eighties with Jimmy Connors, Bjon Borg, and John McEnroe battling it out on TV long ago. Atlanta has held onto the tennis boom long after it has died out elsewhere and continues to have many tens of thousands of people playing every week, which included Cathy back in her single days. In fact, Atlanta still has a doubles league called Ups and Downs, where a tennis player in a wheelchair teams up with a person with two healthy legs and then they square off against another team with the same setup.

Cathy would play and play until she was exhausted and then take apart and collapse her own wheelchair, removing each wheel one at a time, and then flipping each, including the chassis of the chair, into the front seat next to her in her new Toyota Celica convertible that she had saved up for, paying cash. This had replaced the Chrysler Lebaron convertible, which had replaced her '66 Mustang! But this Toyota convertible was her dream car, with leather seats and after-market wheels. Cathy looked good in it with her sunglasses on, and she knew it. This would be the last convertible car she would own because further down the line, she finally had to get the dreaded "van," but that will come much later!

After a few years in Atlanta living this fun, single, jet-setting, world-traveling lifestyle, she started to not feel very good at all. She was feeling run-down all the time and was having to take more and more sick days from work and stay home instead of flying off for meetings or pleasure trips. It was not good. And she did not know why, and this scared her. But one of the doctors at the Shephard Spinal and Rehab Center referred her to the nearby Emory Spine Center, which also happens to be a unique Atlanta institution carved out of the world-renowned Emory University Teaching Hospital.

Cathy continued to become very ill again, and she was diagnosed with major infections growing near almost all of the major organs and into her spinal area. The infections were growing at an alarming rate, and her body was in danger of going into sepsis or cardiac failure. Fortunately, she met Dr. Whitesides and Dr. Horton there at Emory, and if it were not for the cutting-edge medicine of these particular doctors and the team at Emory Spine Center, Cathy surely would have died soon thereafter. Dr. Whitesides devised a surgical plan involving several doctors, one after another, in the same room, applying their surgical techniques to cut open and move around Cathy's precious organs and to "scrape off" layers of infected flesh near her spine.

The doctors were not sure she could even survive such an invasion of her body. But you know what? She did. Cathy survived the back-to-back grueling thirteen-hour surgery and began a long road of recovery that took a few months to come back from. She did this by herself at home once again, but with a mountain of friends and moms of friends dropping by to check on this wonder woman! Even Cathy's mom, Mary, who was doing well in California, was able to take time off and come stay with her some. But this was in the nineties before home health care would become as popular and cost effective and standard as it is now. So mostly, it was Cathy doing the recovering on her own, at home alone with Bailey the cat nearby.

Friends at her company, long before Kick Starter or Go Fund Me, started a campaign there to have coworkers donate money and to reward Cathy their unused sick days and personal days so that she would not use all of hers up or lose any of her pay that she desperately needed. And once again, Cathy slowly began to heal and to actually thrive again, slowly but surely, like a phoenix in her workplace and in her life, all with her undefeatable spirit and faith and with the help of great friends and family.

Cathy always appreciated the help she received from family, friends, and strangers; she just did not always know how to show it or say thank you sometimes enough. But then again, this was the stubborn, proud Norwegian strength that she inherited that helped her get through all the depressing times, and the discouraging times, and even the physically embarrassing times that she would sometimes share. She had a lot of independent pride, which would sometimes come off as selfish or self-centered, but as her brother Randy commented one day, she had to be that way or else she would have never made it through all the ordeals that she and her family went through. But she knew it all was a blessing, and everyone felt good helping Cathy Swenson, who everyone admired for all that she was and seemed to overcome. She always beat the odds, and she was a miracle.

Cathy was ready to have some fun again for a change after recovering. About this time, her friend and coworker Patrice planned a party for all of Patrice's single friends, which in the professional business world can oftentimes be a whole lot of professional single women. These girls were formidable business leaders and were focusing on their careers instead of some future family life. Who can blame them? They were having fun and gaining respect in this new business world; think of the TV shows *Friends* or *Seinfeld.*

Mom Mary, brother Steven and Cathy, circa 1986

*Cathy with her first family, brother Randy, sister Maureen,
brother Steven and Dad, Pete, circa 1995*

Traveling girls...Linda, Mary and Cathy, circa 1997

Cathy with Charlie early dating, 1998

Engagement Party, Cathy and Charlie, 1999

Cathy, being mom, and young Michael, circa 2010

Mary, Maureen, Cathy, cousin Curt,
and Aunt Margaret, in Florida, 2015.

Madrid, Spain with Dad and Eva, 2002

CHAPTER FIFTEEN:

When Charlie Met Cathy

This is when Cathy and Charlie met. It was at Patrice's share-the-wealth party, which is a gathering where you bring a single friend who you are not involved with or necessarily interested in. Patrice, who Charlie knew through a previous girlfriend, invited, and even sponsored Charlie. As a matter of fact, Charlie would not have even been invited to that fateful party if he had not run into Patrice at a Ziggy Marley reggae concert just a month earlier. Come on, that was a God moment, and we all know it!

Now when Charlie arrived at the party with his buddy Steve he did not know what to expect since he hardly knew this group of friends very well at all. Cathy would say later that she had no expectations either and both had stopped even trying to meet someone but to just go with the flow and live life. In fact, Charlie's parents had just that year bought three cemetery plots: one for mom, one for dad, and…wait for it…one for Charlie! They did not want him to be alone for eternity, they said! Sweet, but O ye of little faith.

In this environment, Charlie was standing around talking when Patrice ran in shouting that her friend Cathy needed help with getting up the steps in her wheelchair and were there any strong guys in the house? Well, of course, there were—that would be Charlie, right? LOL. Anyway, Steve and Charlie rushed out to help this friend of Patrice's by each grabbing a side of the wheelchair and proceeding to lift her up, He-Man style! But wait…Cathy turned and yelled directly at Charlie, while surrounded by at least a dozen onlookers, "Don't grab my wheel. You're going to DUMP me out on the GROUND!" And *that right there* was the beginning of Cathy and Charlie's relationship!

Well, everything went back to normal at the share-the-wealth party as the wealth flirted, drank, and sized up each other. Charlie found himself on the back deck talking with someone, not sure who, when he heard the loveliest, sweetest voice he had ever heard floating in the vicinity nearby. He turned to see whose voice was sweetly wafting about…why it was that "girl in the wheelchair" who kinda yelled at him. Interesting. So, she owned a nice and sweet voice, too, to go along with that sergeant one. Huh, the one that had kinda embarrassed him in front of the whole world. Although she was right—it would not have been good if she had been dumped on the ground. Just saying. And wait, aren't those the bluest and prettiest eyes, owned by that same girl in the wheelchair, who was pretty strong-minded, too?

You may have guessed by now that the Charlie in this story is me. Well, I knew I had to talk to her. I mean, really talk to her.

As her previous conversation ended with someone who I don't remember at all, I walked up smiling and firmly shook her hand and reintroduced myself to her. I talked to her and talked to her and talked to her. Cathy was kind of relieved and impressed a little that I had just gone to Europe that year, since she casually stated that she had been many times. We talked about our impressions of London and world traveling. (I had also recently been to Alaska—a different world!) She had traveled a lot more than me, but I *could* hang and I could relate to what she was talking about with my limited but growing travel experiences, and we were definitely building something in common.

We both had great friends and family, and we both liked tennis. We both were polite and respectful to our world and to others (kind of), along with generous opinions thrown in by both of us. It was almost like an episode of *Friends* without the laugh track! It was plenty to show that we both had a commonality and similar backgrounds and a similar mindset. But then my buddy Steve tapped me on the shoulder, saying we must leave now and meet our other buddy, James, at another location as earlier planned. There weren't many smartphones at this point in time to change the agreed upon locations or set plans. Plus, did I want to risk wearing out my welcome with this woman I was clearly attracted to and interested in?

I went back to the angelic and beautiful and inspiring girl, Cathy, to get her phone number. But she was surrounded by a dozen people again. What was with these people? I chickened out of asking her due to the crowd swarming around us and instead went for the firm handshake, the smile, and the sincere, "IT IS SO GOOD TO MEET YOU! My friend and I have to be somewhere. Hope to see you again. Bye-bye."

Well, the hookup for burgers with our friend James was about as uneventful and short as you can imagine. Why did I leave the girl? How could I go out with this cool and different girl? I kept talking to my buddy Steve about her, and then about two days later, I got a voicemail from Patrice.

"Hi, Charlie, this is Patrice. There is someone from my party who wants to go out with you." Who, who I said to myself. It's Cathy…. Wait, wait…which one? Patrice has a sister *and* a friend named Cathy who were *both* at the same party! The recorded message continued, "Call me, and I will give you her number." But *which* Cathy? I kept wondering.

Well, the suspense was killing me, but fortunately I reached Patrice on her phone on the first try, and I (very manly) said, "Hello, Patrice, this is Charlie…so CATHY wants to go out with me?" Patrice's answer was perfect. She said, "Yes, MY FRIEND Cathy says she would like to go out with you if you want to." YEAH, it was the right Cathy, our Cathy!

Cathy, a little later, repeated often that the *firm* handshake was what sealed it for her when we first met that very night. Really? What about the million-dollar smile or the magnetic personality or the great LOOKS? Nope. She always would tell me that it was the firm handshake that reminded her of her father and that it showed I was my own man. Well, I'll go along with that!

Back to Cathy's unfolding lifetime story. Cathy and I had a great first date a week later at our soon-to-be favorite Thai Restaurant (with many, many more dates to come quickly after that). We were already inseparable. We hit it off from the start and my southern family immediately took this California sweet angel under their wing.

However, there is always that first meeting with the prince's parents, the cared-for only son. How would it go, since it was a slightly different situation and everyone knew it—particularly Cathy? Charlie Sr. had always lovingly had a wish that I (Madison, as he called me by my middle name) would hopefully be the last grandson able to carry on the Hairston name, since all the rest were girls. With one last hope for a grandson through a "traditional" family, my dad held onto this dream. Nothing bad. Families from Africa to China to Europe have had this same request since the beginning of time…and even before!

Any thoughts or discussions of THAT went FLYING out the window as Sally and Charlie Sr. were immediately enraptured with Cathy's inspiration, integrity, and by the grace and beauty with which she carried herself. As Charlie Sr. said right after their first encounter with Cathy, "I LIKE your girl!" It was nothing but UPWARD from there in our loving and growing relationship as we grew with each other hand in hand. And Cathy would one day figure out a way to help answer those ancient family prayers and hopes with an intriguing and creative answer that would pave a way for the family name to continue and to be blessed in a new and different way in the process. But that would have to wait a bit.

Then, just a few months after that, Cathy and I traveled back to California together. Cathy's best friend, lovely Linda, as they affectionately call her, was getting married to the love of her life, Landon. Cathy was thrilled to be chosen as the traditional maid of honor, even though her wheelchair showed that she was something different and amazing! In the ceremony, she would, in fact, come down the aisle in her wheelchair slowly and humbly, with all the grace and beauty that you would expect from *any* maid of honor…particularly from Cathy!

This California trip also gave Cathy a chance to introduce me to her whole family. Imagine that! Both sides of this wonderful, blended family came around and were in and out of Mary's or Pete's different houses to be together with her and the new guy. Cathy's protective and deeply caring younger brother, Randy, called Cath and said, "What's this about a guy? Who is this guy?" When I introduced myself and talked alone, one-on-one, with Randy the very next night at Cathy's childhood home in their mom's living room with the Christmas tree beside us, one of the first things from Randy's mouth was, "Hey, no matter how long you two are together or whatever you go through with her health and all, just realize that it will NEVER equal all that we went through as a family. Never."

And he meant it. He let me know in REAL terms what all paraplegics, quadriplegics, and their families go through in their ordeal, and that is: THIS is serious business. Although Randy may or may not even remember this, I never forgot that conversation. It made it clear to me that this was no game. All these lives, particularly Cathy's, had been tested by fire, and they had been brought through it by the grace of God.

Before we returned to Atlanta, we flew to Breckenridge, Colorado to hang out with Cathy's dear friends, Jeremy and Lisa, along with Simon and another British colleague and friend, as well as his beautiful soon-to-be wife and her small children who became their children! It was January 15 and snow season. Breckenridge had the Christmas winter lights still up. The next morning, Cathy AGREED (probably reluctantly) to go SNOWMOBILING. Wow. Here we go!

What a great memory for Cathy! She was fitted for a helmet and snowsuit just like everyone there and went through the same orientation that was required for each participant. She was not going to be stopped. She also did it because she believed that she could do anything, though she just wanted to go a little slower. But the tour leader and guide would not allow us, together on one snowmobile, to go any slower. He had an attitude and seemed to act like she did not really belong out there. What a jerk. But Cathleen enjoyed the snowmobiling immensely with herself in front and me snugly behind her on the banana seat that was kind of like a motorcycle seat. I held Cathy tightly between my legs, using them like a vise grip to keep Cathy carefully in place! In turn, Cathy had a stranglehold on those handlebar grips like nobody's business. She was not going anywhere as long as the snowmobile stayed upright. Fortunately, the paths were mostly clear of heavy snow, which had been ridden and driven all day. Still, it was risky, much like the scuba diving almost fifteen years earlier. Another adventure for Cathy, but did she know what she was getting into? Our girl was always courageous, but never crazy.

The guide and lead driver kept waving at Cathy and me to go faster and faster, but Cathy wanted to be careful. The guide swung back around to us, saying, "Come on…you've got to keep up!" We tried, but with Cathy still taking it nice and easy as we climbed higher and higher along the wide road circling the ridge around the mountain. It was stunningly beautiful and rugged, and she was enjoying every minute. The views across the valley were wintery, although Cathy could only glance quickly.

As we made our way further up, the snowfall got heavier and heavier as we reached the pinnacle of this medium-sized mountain. It was the top of the peak, although flat, and the snow falling around our faces was beautiful and cold but started to obscure our vision. It was stunning but a little hard to see. We slowed down more as we pulled to a stop. Just then, the head driver said, "All right…Let's GO!" The rest of the group took off like they were on fire and they were gone!

Cathy said, "Oh well" and slowly started puttering and turning around, but the snowfall had turned into buckets and buckets of white stuff everywhere. It was blinding all of a sudden… and suddenly Cathy was snow-blind. We could not see beyond the orange suits we were each wearing. What happened? Where do we turn to go? Where is the edge of the mountain? Cathy said that she was just going to wait. We just stopped and waited for what seemed an eternity but was only five minutes. Still, it was freezing cold, and we were starting to wonder how would they find us? It was that blinding. Then, just a couple more minutes later, the snow slowed down a little and the head driver came roaring up beside us. "Come on!" he said. Again, what a nerd.

With pleasure, she thought, and we followed him back to the group, who was waiting for us on the wide ridge road pointing back toward the valley! Hooray, she thought. The group headed back again at high speed, with Cathy driving the snowmobile from the rear of the pack.. Once again, we fell way behind the group and could barely see them anymore. Cathy reluctantly gave up the gas throttle to me when I said that we had to keep up with the group or we could get lost or stranded again. Cathy yelled, "Okay, but slow down." "I can't," I croaked, "or we could get lost again. We need to follow them on the trail to see where the potholes are. I GOT YOU." You know what? I did have her, and I held onto her for good from then on, and she held me in her heart now.. What a trip to Colorado.

Later that same year of dating, Cathy and I traveled together on a trip of a lifetime to Rome, Italy, but first we landed in the South of France where we stayed with her dear friends Jeremy and Lisa, again, near Valbone, which is a village that goes back to 1010 AD. With Jeremy and Lisa now living in a small, but upscale, two-story house, I had to carry Cathy up and down the stairs, since our bedroom was in the basement or ground level. No one batted an eye, particularly me or Cath. It was getting to be normal, and we were both younger and skinnier, so gravity was a little more in check…but it was still a workout!

After a few days, we rented a car, said goodbye to our dear friends, and drove down the coast to the rich people's paradise and multi-million-dollar yachts of Monte Carlo, Monaco. We saw breathtaking views and cities built on giant cliffs off the old Mediterranean Sea wall, used by mariners since Egyptian and Roman times. At each hotel stop, the views were even better, but the steps were getting higher and higher for carrying Cathy and the elevators tinier and tinier. Thus, this was Europe before adding amenities for handicapped people. Cathy would hold firmly onto my neck while I carried her to get wherever we needed to go! But, other times, she would have to wait patiently, sometimes hot and exhausted on the tour bus, while the other tourists and I marched through the Roman ruins or some other impenetrable part of the city, which goes back to the nearby Etruscans around 750 BCE.

Then again, if there was a way, there was a will… Cathy's will. Once we all arrived at Rome's Saint Peter's Basilica, which is a huge cavernous cathedral at Vatican plaza, sitting atop about twenty long granite steps, she was emphatically told by the old school tour guide, "You cannot come with us; you must wait here." Back in 1999, at least, there was no visible ramp for the physically challenged, but Cathy was on a mission. She wheeled her way around this building and spied a back entrance on the far side of this massive building where some monks in robes were waving her in, and rejoined the group inside. But this was just as our tour group was finishing up inside the cathedral and leaving the huge structure.

She asked the stubborn and unsympathetic tour guide if he would please quickly show her around the Renaissance artwork, but he said, "*No*, we are leaving now." I offered to show her the exhibits quickly and was told, "You have five minutes or the bus is leaving without you both!" Well, Cathy and I wheeled around quickly and looked again at the artwork of Michelangelo and DaVinci and then headed for the stairs to go downward. As I tipped Cathy's wheelchair back and started confidently descending, all twenty of the granite stair steps jolted Cathy as she held on with all her strength as the wheelchair was leaned back more and more…kerplunk, kerplunk, kerplunk, kerplunk, kerplunk… it continued…kerplunk, kerplunk …Cathy and I descended in record time and felt each and every jolt and then finally we were safely on the plaza! But the bus was across this park-sized Vatican Plaza, and the bus was blowing its horn. Was it starting to move?

No time to wait—onto the smooth but ancient brick surface of the piazza it seemed safe to let Cathy roll and roll as fast as I could pull her like a tow truck. She said not to worry, that she would be okay and would not fall out… hopefully. I pulled her and pulled her as her wheelchair went flying across the area the size of three football fields, and I ran with her hand extended out into mine. Then I decided to propel her forward with a slinging motion similar to throwing an Olympic shotput…except this was our Cathy!

But it was okay, she thought. Then Cathy started using her own hands to propel the wheels even faster, like she was paddling a canoe from side to side to keep her speed and momentum and correct direction going and was a little ahead of me, with the bus still almost a football field away.

"Look out!" I yelled to a huge group of Japanese tourists just ahead of us and, right on cue, these wonderful visitors all parted right in the middle, just like the parting of the Red Sea. Moses could not have done it any better. Of course, it was really God, anyway. Cathy sailed right through the middle of these nice people and was at the bus in record time. A new Olympic record!

However, the tour guide was not as impressed with this spectacle of paralympic sport and determination as everyone else was. He frowned and sneered, but everyone else on the bus smiled and a smattering of applause seemed to come from way in the back of the full bus. Then after each stop, a dozen of these same bus riders would wait at whichever cathedral or monument or restaurant steps that needed to be negotiated by Cathy and me and were there to help the two of us in every way that they could for the rest of that glorious day. Who says people don't care? You just have to appeal to their kindness and greatness, not their guilt, along with sharing your warm smile. We both had a great time. Cathy was living *life* to the fullest.

CHAPTER SIXTEEN:

It Was Going to Happen

It was going to happen...Hallelujah! Cathy stuffed the wedding invitations into the envelopes, licked each adhesive, and filled out the addresses one by one—from the latest hospital bed that she had to endure. It was some manageable UTI or a bladder stone, which would occur semi-annually for a few years. But Cathy had it under control by now and I did not bat an eye. I just knew she would always bounce back, and she easily did on this and was back in her home and at work in a few days, all after a few IVs and antibiotics got her back on track. Again, no biggy we thought, and we were right.

We married on May 14, 2000, with the service at Redeemer Lutheran in Atlanta and the reception at the old Whitlock Inn near the scenic square in downtown Marietta, GA. Everyone of love and importance came from everywhere, including California of course, but also France, Georgia, Kansas City, and right there in Atlanta.

Even Jeremy and Lisa came over from the South of France to return the love from her attending their wedding a couple of years back. After a short but sweet honeymoon, I moved right in with Cathy, since she already had a comfortable one-story home that was flat on the ground and already easily accessible for her. Everything in the kitchen was on the bottom shelves within easy reach, as you might imagine for a paraplegic. Everyone else had to get on their hands and knees occasionally to find a rear pot or pan or dish, but hey, that's okay…and it's good exercise!

Of course, the bathroom doors and shower entrances were flat and wide enough for accessibility of a wheelchair. Cathy had already had a natural gas grill installed with a natural gas pipe to it so that it would never run out of fuel and was level with her wheelchair. All of this was on her completely accessible and comfortable patio deck outside. She had worked hard, and she was doing okay, even very well, some would say.

Cathy and I loved our new married life. On the one hand, it was a match made in heaven, just like any other good marriage between two people who love each other very much and want to spend their lives together. On the other hand, it powerfully showed that Cathy was just like anyone else, wheelchair or not, who wanted a full life and worked for it while overcoming her obstacles. She dreamed, prayed, and believed, and she had so far been blessed with her own house, a home, a married life, and, hopefully, one day, children, if that was possible. God willing.

As newlyweds, Cathy and I spent lots of time back in
California with her family and friends and her nieces and
nephews, still dreaming of having children of our own.
We went to Las Vegas to see her family there, including
mother Mary, who was doing great with her husband Don,
and Pete and Eva who came at other times. And there were
meet-ups with Maureen and Steve or Randy, her sibs. In
fact, Maureen got married to her husband, Gator (Greg!),
there on one of those trips to wonderful Sin City with all
of the family from California looking on. Cathy's mom,
Mary, was known to have said that Cathy had never been
so happy in all her life.

Well, about this time, just one year into our happy
married life, Cathy noticed a skin issue that would not
go away and kept developing and growing where she sat
against the left wheel of her wheelchair. It is a common
concern for anyone who is bedridden or confined to a
wheelchair. It was on the side of her hip near this wheel,
and being paralyzed, she could not feel it cutting into her
skin nor turn enough or adjust her body enough to allow it
to stay clear or heal properly as it kept expanding. She tried
to deal with it by herself for months, but she knew she had
to see what could be done.

We both were worried about it. So, it was back to
the Shepherd Spinal Center to see what could be done to
alleviate this growing and invasive wound. After a quick
look, the wonderful skin doctor cleaned out the wound with
a scalpel right in front of us and with no local painkiller,

since Cathy could not feel it anyway. She could see him working deeply inside her body, yuk, and we both could hear the excruciating sound. He finished and sent us home, but the wound kept growing, and we were back to see the skin doctor within a couple of weeks. Well, the good doctor took one look and said, "There is no time for us to waste. I am checking you in now before this infects your whole leg."

Before an hour was up, Cathy was whisked upstairs and into a special bed in the Shephard Center, with a groaning motor to control the specific airflow into the mattress so that it reduces the pressure points that so many older people and paralyzed people have to deal with on a continuous basis. Cathy looked at me and we both cried a little. We had just gotten married; it's not fair, I said.

Cathy then looked slowly off into the distance, as she had done probably so many times, staring out the large hospital room window like she was in a trance or something. The sun was *still* shining brightly in the window and on her face.

But then, just as quickly, she immediately turned her gaze back toward me and to my intense and questioning face. She looked at me squarely and intently and said, "God NEVER gives us more than we can handle. Never!" She said this as if it came straight from her wise heart and maybe even from heaven.

Cathy continued, "Nothing is EVER placed in someone's lap that they cannot handle...nothing. Even if someone has a mental or emotional or a physical challenge, God will not put something in front of them that they cannot handle. The Spirit will always give you a way FORWARD. Love will always provide an answer, if we will just seek and accept the answer given to us!"

Not for the first time and definitely not for the last, Cathy reassured her partner, friend, and love that it would be okay. "I will get out of here," she said. And, you know what? She did—two long months later!

In those days, they shared four to a room upstairs at the Shepherd Center, and Cathy was the leader of all kinds of roommates in her big room. All with many different ages and situations, but mostly all involving car accidents that had caused broken hips or fractured pelvises, immediate paralysis, or all of the above. One young lady, Molly, was also mentally and emotionally challenged. Cathy would reassure her roommate Molly over the months with the grace and patience of an angel that everything was going to be all right and that she was there for her. Some nights, Cathy would help talk her to sleep while talking herself to sleep in this dark but noisy hospital ward, saying, "Everything is going to be okay, Molly," into the wee hours of the dark night. And sometimes Cathy would have to cry her own self to sleep because it was that depressing. But Cathy could see the light at the end of the tunnel once again, and she stayed focused on that light.

Cathy got out after about nine weeks and went home, back to work and a career that she had worked at now for almost twenty years. She shook off this latest ordeal and away we drove to Albany to have dinner with my family to celebrate the recovery of both Cathy and my own dad from heart surgery. The Georgia heat and humidity were stifling down south of the gnat line, even after the sun went down, but nobody seemed to care about the heat, including Cathy, who was just glad to be living fully and working and traveling again. Nothing, she thought, was going to stop her. Life is so good. Thank you, Lord. And the ups of life continued on with only a few downs.

The next adventure was a once in a lifetime planned trip to Spain and Morrocco with Pete and stepmom Eva. I had been taking Spanish lessons for years and wanted a place where I could IMMERSE myself and use my second language. Yeah right. I mauled the language at every twist and turn from Madrid to Marbella…the Spaniards are still talking about it!

But one of the standouts of the trip was the altitude-gaining bus ride up the mountains to the Valley of the Fallen, which is a huge granite memorial and cross that honors thousands and thousands of people killed and persecuted during the Spanish Civil War—the precursor to World War II.

Well, on the long bus ride from Madrid and then up the long winding highway up into the mountains, the tour guide announced that the bathroom facilities were broken and not in use. "You will have to wait until we get to the top of the mountain, and then you will be allowed a brief time to use the facilities." Wow, gee… thanks!

So, when we quickly unloaded Cathy's wheelchair to go see the monument, we were rudely told by the tour guide that we were running behind and would only have fifteen minutes. "So if you need to go to the facilities, you better go now or we will leave you!" But Cathy had not seen the valley and the monument, and that would take ten minutes. "Ma'am, if you do not go to the facilities now, we will leave you!" What is it with these tour directors?

Well, Cathy's stepmom had heard enough, and she told the bus driver and tour guide that "you will NOT leave her or us behind…and SHE will take all the time that she needs!"

But Cathy, Pete, and I still felt under the gun and rushed like crazy to get Cathy to the one and only ladies' room… and now what? The door was too narrow? Great… But no problem, Pete declared! "Charlie, you hold up her chair with one of your arms, and then use your other arm to pull one of her wheels off, and then shimmy her chair back and forth until we can get it through the doorway." It worked!

Now Pete and I had to deal with the fact that we, too, were standing in the middle of the ladies' room and women were walking back and forth and in and out. Some cared, but most did not even notice. Still it was awkward, of course.

And then we found out there were no accessible stalls, and the doors to these areas were also TOO SMALL! So, Pete excused himself and left it all to Cathy and me. So, I helped by blocking the view and ran interference for my girl, Cathy, so that the rest of the world could not see what was not to be seen. Mission Accomplished.

But there were still issues getting Cathy back on the Greyhound sized bus, so Pete and I just picked Cathy up together—one on one side and one on the other side. We got her into her seat and the wheelchair collapsed and secured as the tour guide and bus driver STARED at us. The bus slowly started to move and pull away, while all of this commotion was finally coming to an end. "Yes," said Eva, "we did it!"

But although thankful for the help, it was a bit too much emotionally and mentally for Cathy, who felt rushed and embarrassed and abused like a child from the whole ordeal. Cathy started sobbing and crying silently in the pitch-black dark next to me quietly in our bus seats. Only I could hear her.

"What's wrong?" I whispered. "We pulled it off together, as a team. We did not let them stop us."

"You have NO idea how I feel," Cathy said to me as she looked intently with her blue eyes moist and wet from tears."

"Yes, I do!" I answered.

"NO, you don't," Cathy said emphatically. "That was so embarrassing, and I feel so abused. You have no idea how I feel." And she was right; it was very embarrassing... and hopefully no one in a wheelchair again, wherever, will ever be treated in that way.

But about a year later, Cathy noticed extra fatigue and some problems with her swallowing. This was cancer number two, and this time, it was thyroid cancer. Our hero would end up having cancer a grand total of five times in her lifetime, but more on that to come. For now, she went to the hospital, but this time finally just as an out-patient, instead of the miserable bedridden stays she had become so familiar with. This time, she recovered in the hospital for only a few hours after the procedure.

The doctor came and told me that everything had been removed, including her whole cancerous thyroid, but that *everything* was all right.

"But, whoa, please back up! Did you say cancerous?"

"Yes, Mr. Hairston, it is cancer, but it's okay."

"Whoa, please, but wait..."

"What, Mr. Hairston?" asked the totally unemotional and detached doctor as he said impatiently, "You don't have anything to worry about, Mr. Hairston."

"I don't?"

"No, like I said, I removed it all. We had radiation, and we removed her whole thyroid. She will be taking thyroid medicine for the rest of her life. Everything is fine. Now, if you will please excuse me…"

"Well, okay, whew," I said. "I guess I will trust you, doc. Thank you for your…uhm…patience and understanding." Cathy got over this bump in the road and started taking her new thyroid medicine, and you know what? Everything was fine.

We soon flew our nieces, Lauren and Cathryn, to France to stay once again and spend wonderful times with Jeremy and Lisa, and now their three wonderful growing children, in Nice, near the Mediterranean Sea. Perfect times! When that trip of a lifetime was over, we turned around and went back to Vegas, this time hooking up with my dear sister, Caree, and my brother-in-law, Mike. Life was good, even though we only lost money and did not win any jackpots to show from the slot machines, which Cathy so enjoyed. She thinks she got that from her mother and her Aunt Margaret.

And then later that same year, we went to Cancun, Playa Del Carmen, and Cozumel, Mexico all on the same big trip, staying in six different exotic hotel rooms. I did all of the heavy lifting, but Cathy was the trooper who handled all of the heaves and hos and all of the bumps in the journeys.

We went to all these resorts, just because we wanted to explore different resorts with their different themes and to find the perfect hotel room. I know it's crazy, but all at the same time. In fact, Cathy tumbled out of her chair onto a nighttime sidewalk after a drink at one of the beautiful poolside resorts but just laughed it off. "I'm good!" And she was. I just scooped her back up into her wheelchair, and off we went to the next bar and restaurant. The heat was hot, but the true *light* was so much stronger. What would be next?

CHAPTER SEVENTEEN:

Here Comes the Stork

After returning to thank Dr. Whitesides again for saving her life years ago and asking him for his advice, Cathy ruled out trying to carry a child. But she cried at home like I had never seen her cry before or since—with deep, huge, painful tears when she felt that no one, including her own dad and mom, understood how much she really wanted to have her own child, even if it was difficult and almost impossible. Even if the child came from another place or another woman's womb.

So, in classic Cathy style and force, she created another spreadsheet and started looking into every country's and even every state's adoption policies to see if any entity would allow her to adopt a child. The rub was that since she was a paraplegic and in a wheelchair, would she be able to care as a mother should care or be able to take care? The answer is yes, of course, but she had to deal with perceptions, and certainly not everyone in every situation can perform as well as another. Standards are standards for a reason. It was not oppressive, but maybe a little unfair. In the end, all would allow for paraplegics, except for Russia and Romania, if memory serves from a couple of decades back. But were these countries just looking out for the child? China and others had a long waiting list. So, it was time to think local.

Cathy had a wonderful, dear friend and coworker named Elizabeth. With her awesome husband, they were foster parents of neglected and abandoned kids who they soon adopted in the same county that Cathy and I lived in. Cathy thought we could do this, but we could start off slow as weekend or vacation fill-ins for full-time foster parents. After two months of training classes, Cathy and I had such great joy filling in and caring for foster kids for a week or two at a time. Wonderful kids like Jonathan, Samir, and Sharif, and others came in and, sadly, out of our lives!

But something was missing. Cathy missed the long-term bonding and felt like her heart was broken each and every time the kids would leave to go back to their original environment. She needed more time to connect and to make it meaningful for her. But first, we had to close on the new house that we had picked out after many years of searching. In fact, Samir and Sharif's mother and grandmother actually showed up at the title closing! The ladies showed up at the attorney's office with court papers waving in their hands, saying that their two handsome boys had just been released to them. They would not wait until after the closing. Well, when these wonderful ladies took one look at Cathy, they melted and just said, "Cathy, you are so amazing. Thank you so much for taking care of our kids." Cathy said thanks, but she wanted her own kids; that was what was on her mind.

In the meantime, Cathy settled into our new home while I went backpacking in Venezuela on a pre-planned trip with friends in South America. Upon my return, we decided it was time to ask for a long-term foster placement with just *one* special child. We gave no specifications, just a child, we said. Maybe Cathy asked for a boy, thinking it might be easier, but then we waited…and we waited…and we waited. Then it happened! Michael showed up, grinning from ear to ear from the back seat of the caseworker's car, who had just called Cathy saying, "We have a boy for you, and it will probably be a very long-term placement." That all turned out to be true, and it was a huge blessing and a new phase for Cathy.

When he showed up, Michael was just two years old. He had on a cute little jean jacket and had been sleeping all the way over in the car seat in the back of the car. When he opened his eyes slowly, he just gently smiled at me. The caseworker did not know it, but she was the stork—she was the stork that brought Cathy a son.

Michael was an immediate blessing in our lives. He was very comfortable in his new surroundings. A nice lady who knew and lived next door to Michael's biological grandmother called up Cathy and asked if she could please come over to see Michael one last time. "Of course," she said. When this nice pastor's wife later arrived, she explained to Cathy and I that Michael was coming from a very unstable situation and, after she had been in our house for less than fifteen minutes, this kind angel planted a bug in my ear. And that was that we should start a family and adopt this young child! Well, okay!

I knew immediately that this was the thing to do, but Cathy was not so sure. Cathy was always the deliberator, the planner, the analyst, and budgeter, and she needed to deliberate a little more! But once she came around to this new idea, there was no stopping her. This was the way that she would get her own family and become a mother, she thought! He needs us…and we need him. Yes, this was the answer to her many prayers to one day have her own family!

So Cathy immediately took the lead on finding an adoption attorney, filling out the mountains of paperwork and learning and relearning all of the regulations and laws that we would need to know to get to the adoption finish line. It took two long years, but the adoption of our son was completed under Cathy's skill and tenacity. We both went before the judge to secure parental rights. Then we all three went before another judge to obtain legal custody, and then adoption, including changing his name to Michael Kyle Hairston. Finally! Michael even got to play with the presiding judge's gavel. It was so beautiful to see the photograph of all three of us together: Michael, who was given a second *better* chance at life through adoption; myself, whose parents thought I would end up just as a bachelor alone; and Cathy, who had been written off as someone living a lesser life in a wheelchair. And yet, here she was holding up her chin high and smiling from ear to ear with *her own* family!

After all this, Cathy worked hard to get him a new social security number by directing me on what needed to be done. If not for her leadership, I admittedly would not have had the patience or the leadership to get all this done. Last but not least, she organized and planned a big neighborhood Adoption Party, with just about every neighbor, friend, coworker, and loved one all coming to celebrate the end of the paperwork and the beginning of a new and bigger family. Even Pete and Eva made the trek out from California. They did not know when they boarded the plane that the happy couple was going to recruit them to help pull off this party.

"But where's the caterer?" Eva asked.

"It's you and me," I sighed.

"Please cook this, and let's GO!" Life was humming fast for Cathy, and she was doing everything conceivable to live her life…wheelchair or not!

CHAPTER EIGHTEEN:

Life Goes On

Well, our girl Cathy dove completely into motherhood and balancing a wonderful family with all its joys and challenges. There were lots of fun trips to Disney World, Sea World, and Panama City Beach coming up with "her guys," Charlie and Michael. I would push and pull the wheelchair wherever it needed to go. "Watch OUT!" Cathy would say.

Cathy now had her own family years after many had quietly (and not so quietly) said that she would never have her own family or that her life would never ever be normal. None of her friends, classmates, or family remembers teasing her about it now, but she had heard it since she became attached to her wheelchair. In fact, Michael, Cathy, and I were all graduates of the Island of Misfit Toys! And *they* were all wrong as usual, but one has to work hard and believe enough to overcome the "*they*" in your life. And Cathy did. She NEVER stopped believing. She was still pursuing her dreams, and there was still much more to come.

Cathleen continued to have surgeries, and cancers still kept coming up, but she and I aggressively fought and won each battle. The latest was the big one to many—breast cancer, which so many women are affected by whether they are in a wheelchair or not. This time it was discovered early on. Cathy had shown such a resiliency in fighting health issues that I hardly worried when she told me about this latest one. I had already seen her live an exceptional life from a wheelchair, and she had already been in and out of the hospital several times since we had met five years earlier. I guess her faith was so strong on overcoming anything health-wise that I just followed her lead on this. She had faith, and this became my faith. Many of us easily forget how much of an effect we have on others around us—particularly our friends and loved ones!

So, we both went to see Dr. York, the cancer doctor who became Cathy's latest hero doctor. He convinced us that Cathy would be just fine with traditional radiation treatment. Well, our Cathy insisted she could drive herself to her own radiation appointments, no problem! And she did just that. She did not even take off any time from work but kept on logging in forty plus hours a week between the office and the home office. Cathy just kept on going and going and did not complain. Everyone, including some of her doctors, said, "Don't bet against Cathy." Yet she was blessed mainly because she had faith in the God of light, love, and spirit. Put simply, God, the Highest Point in the Universe! She believed in God and herself to overcome lots of things—maybe she believed in overcoming everything.

Our wheelchair-bound Cathy heroically overcame each day by doing many things that you and I do each day and take for granted. One of these things that she accomplished every day was simply getting in and out of her snazzy convertible sports car that she was proud to have. Cathy had almost hero status at Redeemer Lutheran Church, where we continued to attend for ten years after being married there by Pastor Deb. As with a lot of large churches, it is a church of almost a thousand people, so it was not unusual for a church member to live in anonymity to the head pastor. But not Cathy—not for long!

The accessible parking spaces were just below the second story office window of this well-loved head pastor of this unique midtown Atlanta church. One day, while staring out of his window, probably looking for inspiration for his next well-thought-out sermon, he found some deep joy and motivation from Cathy. Pastor Sims confided in Charlie that he had never seen anyone with so much patience in his life.

From his upstairs office, he had one day noticed a sharp-looking convertible sports car pulling into the handicapped spot below him. Hmm…who was this visitor? After a few moments, the driver's side door opened and a big skinny wheel (?) was quickly thrust to the pavement. Interesting, he thought. Then, after a long moment or two, half of a wheelchair came flying out of the driver's side and was guided by two long taut arms as it fell with gravity to the ground. Plop...it crashed slightly. It fell quickly but still in a controlled manner by its owner. Hmm, he thought. So this is how.... Then these arms started pushing some large valve on the wheel, which allowed the wheel to reconnect with the axle on this large chassis. Another wheel then came flying out of the car and onto the ground as these strong arms seemed to blunt its crash. Slowly, that wheel was eventually attached to the bulk of the wheelchair as the metal first scraped and scratched on the pavement. As one taut arm steadied this device, another long arm pulled and pulled to get the back support to come up so that it had a back and looked like a small sporty wheelchair! But wait, there was more....

Just then a very large thick black cushion came flying out of the car and onto the top of the chair...wham. After a lot of adjusting and proper shifting of this cushion occurred, a large shiny board (called a slide board) appeared from the sports car and a person started shimmying across like they were walking the plank of a pirate ship, except sitting down, and for what seemed like a small eternity. After ten to fifteen minutes, this person was finally starting to wheel towards the door. Who was this amazingly determined person? Why, it's that nice woman in the wheelchair from the Outreach Committee! We talked after the last meeting for the first time. What's her name? I know it. I know it. Her name is Cathy!

And Cathleen would demonstrate her patience and

independence, doing this same physical routine for about forty years. That is, until her rotator cuffs in her shoulders were torn to shreds from so much use as she thrust herself in and out of her wheelchair. But she could not stop to let them heal because then she would have to get out of the wheelchair and out of her routine and into a bed for three months or longer. But, hey, Cathy would have it no other way. Not until her strength and her shoulder blades told her that enough was enough! Then, and only then, did she resign herself to getting the usual "Handicapped Van" with its ramps and hydraulic lifts. She was not crazy about it because she had always prided herself on having a normal car that she could control. But it was all okay, too. The hydraulic van helped her keep going when her upper body told her she could not. The van kept her independence going strong, all the way—almost—to the very end.

CHAPTER NINETEEN:
Family Life

Cathy loved being a mother and found great joy and purpose in everything that she did to make Michael's life as good and stable and loving as possible, just like any other family in history. But she still did not believe in being a helicopter parent—you know, hovering all the time. She was looking for balance. She quickly had to learn to deal with these ups and downs of having a child with all of the responsibilities, just like all of us do. It's not easy being a parent or else anyone could do it! Having a child diagnosed with attention-deficit hyperactivity disorder (ADHD) at an early age (kindergarten!) made Cathleen realize that she needed to be proactive and as protective as she could be of her new child and family. Some people or loved ones would say things like, "That boy is just so lucky to have y'all." Really? But aren't all children blessed and lucky to have their parents, no matter where they came from? And aren't we all lucky we had our parents—most of us, anyway?

Today, Michael has now made his mother very proud

and has turned into a wonderful young adult. The sky is the limit! But she still had to deal with the challenges, just like many families do, and Cathy took the lead on deciding what was needed and how to guide our child, how to educate and how to live, just like anyone else—wheelchair or not. It's still all the same. Be a mom. Be a dad. The wheelchair just makes it a little harder. Just saying.

We were both working full-time with lots of success and enjoying the bliss and challenges of our new family, along with vacations and trips back to California, and maybe a few side trips to Las Vegas, which was always Cathy's favorite getaway destination. Growing up, and even into young adulthood, she and her family had always enjoyed getting away from Los Angeles and exploring the sights and sounds of Las Vegas, along with a few slot machines or card games! Swimming pools, movie stars—you know, like the Beverley Hillbillies!

Anyway, our determined role model's career was still ascending and growing. She was looking for new advancement, and so she followed a coworker away from her longtime employer, which was Worldspan, where she had been for almost fifteen years. She had gained so many friends and coworkers there, but she followed this coworker, hoping for greener and brighter pastures. But it did not happen that way. Just then, the whole financial sector started to crumble and the banking crisis started the Great Recession. So, this coworker and Cathy both went to a smaller upstart in the travel industry that really was not the best fit for Cathy. It *was* great pay but much less stable and more of a contract position. As the Great Recession of 2008–2010 started kicking in and threatening economic growth, she found herself being the first laid off from this job. Several more jobs and ever-changing contract positions were to follow for the next few years. It got scary for her and the family.

Cathy and I were both still working, but Cathleen was still the main breadwinner in the family. Each of these positions would now only last for about six months at a time, and even these contract positions were starting to dry up as well. And just then, with the banking and mortgage industries on the verge of collapse, Cathy found herself unemployed.

I, the husband, was still working in the mortgage banking industry, which was one of the main, if not the very, industry pulling everything down. It was stressful with a banking meltdown and recession lingering, and then I lost my income and my job as the mortgage industry imploded.

With all of this going on, she still needed good health insurance and short-term unemployment pay due to the ongoing health issues and medications that she was taking. The health insurance from my past provider was long gone as well. The company that had just laid her off was contemplating whether they should even honor their share of her Cobra health insurance, which is the in-between-jobs health insurance program in many states that is still astronomically expensive—but oftentimes is still the only lifesaver out there for many people going through layoffs. There has got to be a better way, people!

The reason that her most recent employer was considering not covering these costs had to do with the fact that, technically, it was a contract job. Technicalities are used by all of us in many situations, including businesses making financial decisions, but that did not help Cathy and her family in this situation. She was relying on this lifesaving health insurance and short-term pay, just as millions of other people have relied on it, in the past and *now*.

Well, her cell phone rang about a week later. It was one of the human resources personnel calling her with an update. This same manger had always liked Cathy and was inspired by her situation and her life.

Well, good news! Her former company would indeed pay their share of the health insurance! They had come to the conclusion to do the right thing and to honor their commitment. This was due to this same human resources manager, who had recruited Cathy, and who kept saying to her bosses, "But you *have* to do this. You *Have* to honor her Cobra health care and unemployment. She is on cancer treatment, and she needs this, and her family needs this!" And you know what? That is exactly what they ended up doing. Thank God! Cathy was so appreciative of this coworker going to bat for her, maybe even putting her job and her own standing within the company on the line, just to do the right thing.

Thank you so much to this angel whose name now escapes us, but whose heart blessed one very grateful family. Thank you, Lord, for Angels, everywhere, who watch over all of us. And sometimes we get to be that *angel* in someone else's life!

So, the woman whose life was constantly changing followed me over from Redeemer Lutheran Church, where we were married and first joined, to First United Lutheran, as I was now serving on staff every Sunday morning as a contemporary musician and leader! Well, she threw herself into her new church, finding committees to join, casseroles to bake, and putting radical remodeling ideas into action, while more importantly, making new lifelong friends, like her new dear friends Linda, Sharon, Martha, and Bev, to name just a few. I seemed to be the praying and spiritual one in the family, while Cathy was always the practical faith in action one! Cathy was the one even more interested in community and people than I was, although that might be a close call.

Well, Cathy was challenged again and again had her second bout with breast cancer at this time, and fourth cancer total so far, and this time she had to buy a wig to cover up the slow but steady loss of her hair as she continued chemo and radiation treatments. She did not bat an eye at doing this and loved the way her "new hair" looked. Some said, "I love your hair" and she would have to be honest and say, "It's actually my wig, but thanks, I love it too!" Once again, she continued working straight through while taking only minimal time off, and she was still driving into the office on most work days back then.

This time, our fighter had to have *all* of one breast and part of the other breast removed. Dr. Grace Maw did the surgeries at Piedmont Buckhead Hospital, which Cathy would become very connected with later. But there were complications, not from the surgery itself, but from the inconsistent turning of Cathy's body while in the hospital. Another deep skin lesion developed that happened while in the hospital. Why did this keep happening?

The lesion grew and grew, and that became the main concern, sending her back to the Shephard Center for skin care and later surgery to sew up the opening. After that, this never-say-quit woman ended up staying at Shephard again for a couple of weeks to recover before it was finally time to come home. Still more and more time in hospital rooms! What a champion! It was time to have some fun again and put these health scares behind her again. She had had enough of hospital rooms!

About this time, Cathleen's mom, Mary, moved out to Georgia and was near Cathy and her family. She probably did this for a new start since Mary's husband, Don, had just recently passed away from a long-term illness. He was a fine man for Mary, but a good bit older. It seemed that Mary wanted to reconnect at a deeper level with her middle child, Cathy, who had gone through so much in so many hospitals before moving away from their California home such a very long time ago. Twenty years ago, it was. It was time to start a new phase of this special mother-daughter relationship.

Cathy continued working hard at her career, thankfully, working mostly from home now at this point. As a mother, Cathy had her share of soft moments and then very stern moments. Sometimes she would be the good cop, and sometimes she would be the bad cop. She could certainly be the disciplinarian that our son needed to stay on track, no matter what would be pulling him in other directions. She never lost faith or gave in to negative situations. She was a strong mother, and a solid, almost perfect wife. Even with her never-ending health challenges and disabilities, she was always the center that held everything together. Nothing could stop her from doing what she knew was right. She could read the Riot Act like nobody's business and have a Come To Jesus Meeting at the drop of a hat!

CHAPTER TWENTY

Stage Four …
Exit Right?

About this point, Cathy was then diagnosed with metastasized breast cancer (stage four). Stage Four is the final stage, but one can keep going for years with the right health care. We fought each bout aggressively, but she started having many complications, yet continued traveling back to California to see her family and friends. This included a wonderful trip to, you guessed it, Las Vegas! We also visited the Grand Canyon, as well as Southern California, to see everyone from her childhood. Cathy could wheel confidently through a casino as well as anybody!

When we returned from California, Cathy agreed to help Sharon, one of our dear friends from church, host a baby shower there at the church fellowship hall for her upcoming first grandchild! Even though this type of party had rarely, if ever, been sanctioned for church use, Cathy said no problem and told the pastor defiantly of her plans to help host this event for her friend's extended family.

There were apparently no questions asked. Cathy was on a mission! She planned everything out, ignored complaints from other *church ladies*, and stayed true to her plan. And it went just fine and was eternally appreciated by Sharon and probably by everyone in her extended family.

At this time, Cathy was helping at church quite a lot, and she felt like it made a difference in people's lives, including her own. She served on church council and ran nominating committees by herself and continued volunteering more and more of her time to run and upgrade the church kitchen and all its responsibilities of preparing food for after-church services, memorials, and all special events. She immediately came up with plans (some startling) to modernize and upgrade the church bathroom facilities and to welcome all to God's house with a bright new look. We can pay for all of this—just follow me, she would be saying with her actions. She did all of this while working full time from the confines and comfort of her trusty wheelchair. She was the boss. She was the Queen of the kitchen.

And she loved planning the specific coffee hours right after church, which she did for eight years, going on nine. She threw herself and her energies into planning every detail and budgeting every dollar for paper supplies and regular food items. She would go in her now hydraulic lift conversion van to wherever it was cheaper: Sam's Club or Costco or Walmart or buy it online—or better yet, sweet talk me, her devoted husband, into picking it up either on my way home from somewhere or "just go now, please!

Thank you!" That was Cathy; it had to be just right.

Cathy said that it was fun for her to plan a dinner party every week, which she had never really done before, and sometimes twice a week if there was a memorial or a happy graduation or a going away party for someone. Again, she was staying busy and not letting the health problems like Stage Four cancer or her disability in the wheelchair stop her! It was constantly in the church bulletin almost every week: please contact Cathy Hairston if you would like to help. Or could help. Oftentimes, people did.

In fact, most of the church admired all this planning and doing, while Cathy was dealing with cancer and holding down a major career job. She was also keeping her family and her son moving forward while being a main supporter of the church—all while living and being paralyzed in a wheelchair. This was not as easy for our Cathleen as it used to be. Time and aging were catching up with Cath, and there were more aches and pains to go along with her 100 percent efforts. But she did not let it slow her down. She kept plowing ahead. Nothing was going to stop her... or was it?

In fact, First United Church quickly went to a parking lot worship service for over two years during the pandemic. But Cathy did not let this stop her from serving the best hot beverages and refreshments you could find. She and Linda, with my trusty help, provided coffee, refreshments, and sweet treats to the congregation after *every* church service for over two years. (And it was only rained out twice in two years!) They set up a tent awning in the cracked parking lot *every* Sunday morning under Cathy's direction, and this became the highlight of the whole day for many. The refreshment hour on steroids!

CHAPTER TWENTY-ONE:

The Hand You Are Dealt

There were still a few trips to Las Vegas left in our girl, including one to meet up with her mom, Mary. Cathy had not seen her mom in person in almost two years, since Mary had moved back to California after living many years in Georgia and Florida. I think good ol' California is where Mary belonged, anyway!

With her wheelchair that was a never-ending shadow in her life, Cathy was also able to meet up with her sister, Mo, plus cousin Shelly and her wonderful new husband, Don. She lived it up in Vegas, if you want to call having a drink and losing $200 in a slot machine wild! But Cathy ended up arranging and taking everyone to see a Rat Pack impersonation show featuring singing actors playing Dean Martin, Sammy Davis Jr., and ol' blue eyes, Frank Sinatra! After having a great get-together and saying goodbye to Shelley and Don, Cathleen, and I rented a car and drove the bright and sunny three-hour trip across the beautiful desert through Cajon Pass to see the family and everyone else in nearby southern California.

Even with all of her own challenges health-wise and physically, Cathleen was determined to get her brother, Steven, and her mom together again. It had been quite a while since those two had been together, with Steve living with his wonderful family up in Central California, known as the high desert, with its soaring heat and high altitudes. Mary had just reached eighty-one and dementia was starting to set in for a long goodbye. So we drove Mary up into the highlands to see Steve, where it was 120 degrees Fahrenheit *that* day! Even with the insufferable heat, we all had a great time reuniting and talking about all those wonderful and dreamy times in California growing up, including the special times with family and friends...and the life-changing event of Cathy's paralysis.

After this side trip to California was complete, Cathy and I flew back to Georgia. It would be the last time Cathy would ever see Mary. For you see, we got a call from sister Maureen just a few days later. Mary had passed away coming back to her bed from the bathroom. At least Cathy and Steven had seen her one last time. This brave woman who had guided and been there for Cathy during some of her darkest days was gone.

Well, Cathy was the one person who wanted to take on the disbursement of Mary's will, the finalization of the estate, and the months-long planning of their mom's military style memorial there in Riverside, California. This military memorial was available because Cathy's stepdad had been a veteran serving in World War II.

She took it all on and prided herself on being the analyst and detail-oriented sister who loved to organize things. Even if people outside the family thought she was disabled, she was far from that. And she was definitely a leader within her greater extended family. Sometimes you did not want to go up against her! If Cathy was pushing or planning something, most of the family on both sides would not want to go against her wishes. You would just try to get your angle into the mix! It was a sign of the deep respect that Cathleen had earned from all that she had overcome in her challenging life. It was good to have her on your side. And occasionally it would indeed rub the wrong way, but that never did stop her from doing what she thought was *right*. She could not help it. She had to be strong. If she did not, she might not have made it this far. She had to be that way to deal with everything she went through and *overcame*. But wherever she was, she was maybe the most able and determined person around. Most people recognized this right away. If they didn't, this strong, proud woman soon helped them to see it!

Cathy planned the internment at the huge veteran's cemetery in Riverside, California mostly by herself. It is the largest veteran's cemetery in the country. She worked out all the details when she was not working her nine-to-five job, and she paid deposits from the other side of the country, often by mail, for a large luncheon at the historic Sycamore Inn, which was an old jail and saloon in Upland, her hometown, that had serviced the old road through the middle of California during the gold rush days of the 1800s and even before with the Spaniards and the multitude of California Indian groups there in that area! It was surrounded by large, graceful sycamore trees harking back to that same era!

The luncheon was a nice gathering of a diverse crowd of relatives, friends, and others who broke bread and toasted Mary together. Many flowers were brought over to the restaurant for viewing after the memorial was done. Cathy had been graciously thanked for planning well.

When everyone was leaving the beautiful old restaurant and saloon, which could have passed for any cowboy movie or TV saloon, Cathy noticed that a huge Tournament of Roses type fixture of flowers was left with no takers. It was like the rose display they give out to the winner of the Indianapolis 500. It was that big—and beautifully given by one of Randy's friends. And it was humongous even for a pickup truck! But there were no takers to lift and carry and drag and drive this lovely monstrosity away from the restaurant. That is where it continued to stand.

But our girl Cathy dug in her heels (or was it her wheels) and would not leave the Sycamore Inn with me or Michael for over an hour while trying to get someone to come take these flowers back over to Maureen's condo.

She called and called all her brothers and sisters to ask who would come get this gigantic standing bouquet of roses. No one answered. They were *huge.* The florist probably used a semi-truck to deliver them! She asked the waitresses if they had a truck. One felt so bad for Cathy that she said she might be able to get them on her day off—next Tuesday! Maureen finally said she would get them, just not today. Ha. When Cathleen left California days later, she was still trying to get that behemoth of giant roses moved to her sister's house, who did not ever want them or get them. But that was Cathy! She would have taken those flowers back to Georgia if they would have let her fit them on the plane!

When they did get back to Georgia, Cathy just kept moving forward and kept going with me close by or usually right there by her side. But she would more and more need to go into the hospital with fatigue or UTIs, so an IV and a short stay and a "tune-up" usually followed, with an antibiotic or two. This time, it was different. The doctors noticed that her blood pressure was crashing to very low levels; two to three times a day, her blood pressure kept dropping. So, they started giving her a pill to have it go back to normal, and it did, usually within thirty minutes.

After keeping her through Thanksgiving and figuring this out, they sent our girl home, where the pills continued to work just fine as they added a new specialist to the roster, but it worked for now. Cathy resumed working her job from home as she continued to build up her pension and retirement plans. She and I were still focused on improving our home and getting lots of improvements done around the house. She wanted to stay busy with everything, including focusing on Michael's life as he entered welding school. She was working and planning with her new friend Linda for many hours each and every week in their beloved church kitchen and the newly remodeled bright and shiny fellowship hall, which Cathy and Linda had spearheaded.

Cathy became somewhat of a folk hero at the church as she continued working, planning, and organizing in the kitchen at church through her illnesses and setbacks. When she was asked why she put SOOO much energy into providing food and refreshment for members and visitors alike *each* week? Cathy answered without missing a beat, saying, "People need to know the love of God and that we *love* them. There is no better way to show God's love than to give people a clean, nice place to worship and where they can get food and refreshment and feel the love. If you feed them, they will *come*!" And do you know many did come for that reason alone? Because of Cathy and her co-leader Linda!

Well, Cathleen wanted to get away right after the holidays for a get-back-to-some-fun trip! And guess where? Las Vegas is where she wanted to go! Imagine that! But she loved the luxury and pampering of the four-star hotels, the lights and the glitz, and the water fountains of the main road known as "the Strip." And she loved those frustrating but so fun slot machines that she had played since her early adult days living in California. So, she and I went back after Christmas and did it again—and we loved it. It was so much fun. Cathy thought this may be the last chance. We even went back to where we saw, a few months earlier, the Rat Pack with our loved ones…and mom Mary! With her heart complications growing, Cathy knew this might be the last romantic getaway together….and sadly, it was.

Well, like a lot of people, Cathleen knew early retirement was coming up soon, but she kept getting up every weekday and logging on to her computer and her job, every Monday through Friday during those long winter and then early spring months. "When do I wave the white flag and say enough is enough?" she thought out loud.

Cathy's physical life was somewhat okay, but it was getting a lot harder for her to live, propel herself in her wheelchair, and she was constantly seeking answers to her health problems but not finding the answers she needed to get her good health back. She was still planning all week long the running of the coffee hour every Sunday with Linda and still loving it! We were still going out to dinner sometimes, but she would oftentimes have to pass up a fun concert in town or a weekend trip to South Georgia to the lake house to see family. She just did not have the energy for it all.

About this time, it all changed for the proud girl in the wheelchair who would not give in to anything. She had to adjust to a new reality. I canceled all of my planned camping trips and never went too far away anymore. Michael would be home to watch out closely for Cathy if I even went for a few quick hours down south to see my side of the family near Albany, GA. I just did not want to be too far away from her for too long ever again. I was not just the loving, devoted husband anymore, but I was now her most trusted *caregiver, as well.* This was difficult for anyone. It was now a fact of life.

CHAPTER TWENTY-TWO:

Retirement . . . I AM Ready!

Well, the health issues had finally caught up with Cathleen, as they do eventually with all of us. Whether we live to be just one or sixty-one or a hundred-one, the body's health issues will eventually tell us and win out on this earth. Heaven and eternity are forever, but the human body is not. Cathy was amazing in how she kept the tiger at bay, in the cage for so long, for over forty-five years! She did it all with phenomenal energy, determination, and grace. And love!

Cathy, the girl who had lifted herself up by her own self, had to retire from her work and career that same spring. "I cannot do this anymore," she said.

She had been proud of her work for over forty years. And she had done all of this and worked her butt off—from a wheelchair at that! But she was not done yet. She started this new retirement journey by going on six months' disability with her company to see if she could still try a comeback. No sooner had she started this new journey, she looked over one bright, shining morning to my side of the bed and said, "Honey, I cannot catch my breath. I think I need to go back to the hospital."

Cathleen went to the hospital, and this time almost flatlined twice while there. It was close. But she rebounded *again* after two weeks—enough to be declared able to be discharged by the doctors. The staff had connected her to oxygen machines when she first got there, and they were now prescribing her to have oxygen tanks 24/7! This was a first and a huge new development for her and for me. The administrators now were pushing to send her to a rehab hospital. (Prescribers always do. It is for profit, after all.) But I said no. "If she goes into that situation, just like with a lot of people, she will probably never come out of it, never come home again. I am plenty strong enough to lift her, turn her, and take better care of her and manage her oxygen tanks than anybody else," I said. And you know what? I did just that! We would have six more good months *together* at home, where she loved being with her family! Instead of living in and having everyone come visit her daily in some cooped up miserable, cold hospital rehab room.

Well, this proud, self-reliant mom was as tenacious and forceful as ever, which I had always loved and admired about her. Though she had always been proudly independent, I knew that I had to help her start making more of these life decisions. "Let me help you and take care of you," I said to her. And she finally did let me help more after protesting some. Except, it still drove her crazy, just like it would all of us. We want to be in control and then we lose control! How ironic is that? But that's why Cathy fought so hard all her life; something was always trying to wrestle control away from her—her health problems, the cancers, the paralysis, the wheelchair, *circumstances*…but she would *not* let it!

CHAPTER TWENTY-THREE

One Last Road Trip!

Cathy went home again, and she got used to the constant rattle and hum of the oxygen tank machine that I rolled every day from the bedroom down to the kitchen and family room area where she would spend the rest of the day watching TV, texting friends, and fixing her many cups of coffee and her own lunch. This was while I was working around the house or working at projects and gigs, musical and otherwise, and working at the voting polls as a volunteer.

Again, she believed in herself and had faith and was still very independent-*minded* at this point, but could not do all the things her mind wanted to be done. So, she started *delegating* what her mind thought needed to be done! To me, Linda, and to everyone else! And in the long run, it was okay and just fine, for we all understood how frustrating this was for this powerful cancer survivor and strong businesswoman who was a paraplegic! And for most of the summer, Cathy could not go much of anywhere except to church and the many doctor appointments with me driving and pushing her still trusty wheelchair and sitting devotedly by her side.

She was now taking about ten pills a day, including the cancer chemo pill, Ibrance. I would often give them to her, but Cathy was *still* the one in charge of it. They were her medications. She knew exactly what to take and when to take it. I did not. Sometimes, when new doctors, nurses, or technicians would look at me as the leader of her health, I would correct them before she would have to say anything. "My wife has been in charge of her health since she was a teenager. She still is." Occasionally, over the years, I would have to suggest better ways or new ideas, and Cathy would reluctantly agree. But she always, to the very end, knew her body better than anyone. Nobody knew better, not even the doctors.

But she still kept a hopeful attitude that she was going to beat this cancer, along with all these other health complications, just like she had always done. Hopeful, that is always the best way to go! She hated the oxygen machines, but she knew she had to have them. Cathleen still had her mind, her will to live, and her sanity, and she still had her faith and trust in God. She knew that her family and loved ones were looking out for her. She knew that her friends and colleagues everywhere were praying for her.

Ever since her mom Mary passed away a year ago in California, Cathy had wanted to do a second and final memorial service for her up in Great Lakes Michigan, where Mary grew up. This is the uppermost northern and most rural part of Michigan called Big Bear, where Cathy's grandfather had once worked at a tavern and inn where an Alfred Hitchcock movie had been filmed. Even though her latest health problems had prohibited her traveling during the last year, she perked up again when talk of this came up with her cousins, Shelly and Curt. Talk started back that maybe Cathy and I could somehow go and do this memorial! We knew this might be the last chance for her ever to travel again in her life.

Well, this talk started to intensify with brother Randy and sister Mo on board to come over from California, along with cousin Shelley and her wonderful husband, Don, who were coming from Wichita Falls, Texas. We all would go back to Michigan's Upper Peninsula to scatter Mary's ashes at the beautiful, tree-lined cemetery plot just off the shores of rugged Lake Superior where two of Mary sister's, Aunt Margaret and Aunt Bev, are also interned and memorialized.

But how could Cathy logistically make this trip? She was doing a little bit better physically, and she had finally qualified with her insurance for a light-weight portable carry air machine. But it only had a battery charge of two to three hours. Would that be enough time with its battery charge to go through two airports along with time in the air? Probably *not*.

Well, Cathleen had always been part of the airline

industry, so her thinking was always about flying, but her sister, Maureen, said, "Why don't you and Charlie just *drive*? It's only two days away and you will have a great time seeing the countryside!" Your wheelchair and oxygen tanks will all fit in the car. Well, duh. We had never thought of that! And that is exactly what we did.

With me as her loving husband and chauffeur, Cathleen took off and traveled one last time to the Great Lakes of Michigan to scatter her mom's ashes and to explore the state that her parents had met in so long ago. She would discover more than she realized about the rural great north where her mother and her mother's twin sister, Aunt Margaret, had lived and where the rest of those siblings had been raised and challenged by events in their own lives. A lot of people we call Californians are actually shaped and raised elsewhere and then are transplanted to California, bringing their values and ruggedness with them. But Upper Michigan is where Cathy's grandfather had once lost half of his arm on one of the many, many hunting trips he took in those beautiful woodlands, usually with the sole purpose of securing food for his family back then—squirrel, possum, you name it! I don't know about you, but that sounds unappetizing to me!

So anyway, Cathy and I took off from Atlanta one fine morning and headed up through the beautiful hills and mountains of Tennessee and Kentucky. We had never had any reason to find out how to charge Cathy's air machine in the car because all we had ever done was go to doctor appointments since she started using it. But we finally figured out how to get the battery to start charging—somewhere around the Ohio border! Cathy, at this point, was the phone and GPS expert of the family, so she would click and swipe and swipe and click while I dodged in and out of traffic, just trying to get basically to the Canadian border in two days' of driving.

Online, Cathleen found a Marriott Courtyard or something in Dayton, Ohio. (Good Day Dayton was the local morning TV show. Cute!) After a nice meal at Olive Garden, we headed to our hotel room. Cathy was indeed exhausted with all of her breathing and heart problems. I had to get a huge cart and roll it up a big incline to get to our floor with all of this heavy machinery. This was after pushing her up and getting her situated first, of course, but it was so worth the muscle aches to have Cathy traveling again.

After this physically challenged, amazing person rode in the car for another ten hours the following day and survived my driving, she and I pulled into and settled into the destination hotel around 11:00 that night. We were finally there in Marquette on the Upper Peninsula of Michigan! We will make plans tomorrow, everyone. We are tired. Good night!

Now, cousin Curt still lives in the upper part of Michigan near Canada, where much of Mary's family still calls home. So, he became the ambassador, planner, and tour guide for this wonderful group of hooligans, siblings, and cousins. On the itinerary first was to visit Uncle Dick, who was the last surviving husband and widower of these four wonderful sisters. He belonged to Aunt Bev, one of Cathy's other aunts that we were going to memorialize on this trip. We made the sunny and beautiful trek back out of the small city and into a little more rural area.

We went by the cemetery that we were told Aunt Bev's ashes had been interned in…somewhere on the grounds. At last, her name was spotted by the group of exploring cousins along a large wall of other names that, sadly, had passed. I guess it is part of life; we live, we die, we live eternally, but what really happens after that? We seek and find the answers to that age-old question so that we are each prepared, along with our souls and spirits. I believe we live forever in spiritual form. We were formed from Spirit. Everything in this universe is energy or spirit. It just changes its form. Water to ice to clouds. Same with us! Ah, but are you a good spirit? A good energy? *That* is the question. Keep working on that heart of gold before it is too late. Then God, which is light and love, will take whatever essence is left. Be a good essence that adds to the love of this universe.

Back to the story. After just a wrong turn or two, our merry caravan advanced down a long, unpaved, grassy road and found a quaint and beautiful spot way up above looking down on the small but snake-like river below. Rugged and peaceful were the words that came to Cathy's mind. And out came Uncle Dick with his humor and his grown grandson.

With his NRA cap on, Uncle Dick greeted our group with hugs and wisecracks and jokes galore. "Hello, dear Sweetie," he said as he reaches down to kiss Cathy, with her oxygen tubes proudly on display as they provided fresh air through her nostrils. After taking tours around the property in his truck and on foot and telling about the land and the river, he settled in around the deck and started yarning stories of Aunt Bev's attempt at fly-fishing, which was funny but at her expense since she was not really the outdoor type! And there was much more family history.

As Randy and Cissy turned on their phones' video cameras, Uncle Dick then started telling the group wonderful and heart-felt stories of Aunt Bev's last days, since Beverley, her given name, was the oldest of these four sisters, and had only died a year ago, just like Mary. In fact, all four sisters died within a year of each other. The fourth sister was another dear sister, Judy, who passed away within a year of her other sisters as well and was buried with her family down in North Carolina.

But that afternoon, Dick told everyone sitting there how his wife had had many health issues the last few years of her life. He sadly and touchingly shared how Bev and he had to decide when to take "that last car ride to the hospital" when they knew that this would be it—the end of the road for Bev's life. I looked over at my dear, strong, super-amazing wife. Dick continued and said that one day Bev made an uncontrolled yelp of pain and a choking sound…and they both knew that this was it.

"Okay," said Bev, "I'll go to the hospital, but can I please just stay here at home? Just one more night, please?" "Sure," he said.

They got up early and went in the next morning to check into the hospital…her last hospital room. The family doctor came in to see Bev where she was lying in this last hospital room. Seeing that she was completely incapacitated, the family doctor gently reached down and slowly started feeding Aunt Bev her ice cream cup that had been brought in with her food tray. The doc fed her one spoonful of ice cream at a time, over and over, as he fed…and fed her… using his own hand, twirling the spoon upside down so that she could lick and enjoy each delicious bite. And Bev licked and licked and loved each creamy cold bite, just like an infant. Everyone knew what this great act of joy and care was about. It was about how no matter what someone's station in life, they could still serve and care for someone else who needed to be cared for. No one is too good to wash someone else's feet or feed them hand to mouth; we are all equal. No one better.

As the tale goes, Bev died shortly thereafter in the hospital room. As Cathleen listened to this sweet but sad story, with her own oxygen machine rattling and working for her while sitting in her wheelchair outside on Dick's patio deck in northern Michigan, Cathy could not help but wonder if this powerful story was not meant to help her— to prepare her for what was coming down the road in her own life.

That night, the cousins all met in Maureen's room and toasted stories of before and after, with challenges and love growing up with their different mothers—the three sisters they would be memorializing early the next morning—their moms. Cathy had been the independent, strong, passionate, never-give-up person who had planned all of this out with the precision, passion, and persistence that she had done with everything in her life.

Anyway, they continued toasting and Curt, Aunt Margaret's son, shared memories of his time in the military so long ago, telling revelations that none of the rest of us there even knew about! Cathy had to excuse herself to bed across the hall in this hotel. She was exhausted from so much but so glad still to be there. Literally. I followed her across the hall, helped her in the room, and lifted her into the bed (barely), and set her up with the large rolling bedside oxygen machine that kept her going all night. I then went back across the hall to continue the stories and celebrating, while closely watching my phone, just in case she suddenly needed me.

The next crisp autumn day, we all made the drive up further north into the high woodlands to the shores of Lake Superior. When we saw it, it looked as big as the

Mediterranean Sea, and it felt as big with its steady waves lapping over the shore. These waves can turn deadly and into near tidal waves whenever the air of November shows up. There are many stories of weather quickly deteriorating on this Great Lake and sinking famous boats like the *Edmund Fitzgerald*, made famous in that haunting song of the same name by Gordon Lightfoot, who sadly just recently passed away as of this writing. In fact, our friend Lonny, who is an avid outdoorsman from central Michigan, and who, still to this day, does not and will not go out in any kind of fishing boat onto Lake Superior. He says it is too unstable with the waves, without a moment's notice, crashing into and rocking the boat from side to side. And the waters are cold all year-round. It is buried with everything from ships to people, hundreds of feet deep. No thank you, he says! But we continued on and we found the beautiful old cemetery where Cathy's grandfather and the other ancestors are buried now along now with the remains of the three sisters.

"You are the closest thing we have to a pastor, Charlie!" So, I led the simple ceremony honoring Cathy's mom and her twin sister, Aunt Margaret and, of course, dear Aunt Bev. Words of hope and family connections and the enduring peace and power of God were shared by everyone. Elvis' "Love Me Tender" was sung with heavenly tears of remembrance and joy for the life and the *loss* of these three beautiful sisters.

Under these beautiful old majestic oak trees, right next to the plot where her ancestors are buried, this group of the living sang, loved, honored, and shared hope for future generations and for those who had come before them. I helped Cathy carefully roll her trusty wheelchair over the twigs and the gopher holes as she crossed underneath these sweeping trees. Her opaque oxygen tubes were ever-present, going into her nose. She still hoped she would get better; enough to get rid of them! I reminded the group with a warm smile to never forget our loved ones. Hold on to their memories and their spirit, and thank God as we each understand the creation. For Cathy, it was through Jesus that she was thankful and was saved and that she had lived with the power of renewal and rebirth all her life.

That same group of cousins that were there sharing life and enjoying that day would be two fewer in just six months. Besides Cathy, Shelly's loving husband, Don, was there under the oak trees, and he would also pass in just over six months. We miss him very much, too. But Cathy still had more living to do after that day, and the church kitchen and fellowship hall were calling her back! She could almost hear it all the way up in the Great Lakes!

This strong, but almost worn out, hero headed back home to Atlanta, ready to continue fighting and beating the cancer…or at least to keep it at bay, she hoped and believed with all of her heart! She was praying to God for every day of her life. She had finally made it to Michigan to return her mom's ashes to her birthplace. Thank God. She had made it! What a last trip.

CHAPTER TWENTY-FOUR:

An Ending . . . and a New Beginning

After being back home for a few weeks, Cathy and I started realizing that her cancer and the many complications of her breathing and heart rate were not getting any better. Throughout the pandemic, Cathleen never caught Covid but always used the same general caution of wearing masks and disinfecting her hands during the two plus years of the pandemic. She got all of her vaccinations as soon as she could. It was the least she could do. She believed in doing the right thing, always. True blue.

But just a few weeks after returning from Michigan, Cathy became more and more bedridden. This still mentally strong, but physically deteriorating, woman could not at this point go into the church anymore to help in person. But she still called in and texted Linda and her friends Martha and Bev at church and everyone on the outreach committee with suggestions for what she thought the church needed to be doing and what refreshments needed to be served!

Where the best bargains for those refreshments could be found! Some things never change. But they do.

I would help her constantly by bringing her whatever she needed. Not just meals, but everything, and often her favorite was a sandwich or salad from Chick-fil-A. We would use our cell phones like a beeper intercom. If I was in the yard or another part of the house, I would see it and would not answer it, but would just head straight back to the bedroom. "Yes, Sweetie?"

When it was time to shower, I would help her slide on the slide board in and out, but it was not easy at all for me, or for Cathleen to balance herself, even with my help. It could get a little frustrating. She started to black out whenever exerting herself. Over a few more weeks, it got nearly impossible for her to do most anything. In time, we agreed she needed to go back to the hospital. "Okay," she said, but she insisted that she get cleaned and showered first. Still full of dignity and independence and wanting to be presentable all the time. But after this or that particular shower, she was so tired and so exhausted that she just had to go back to bed...maybe try again tomorrow to go back into the hospital. It seemed that Aunt Bev's story about that final ride to the hospital that we had just heard in Michigan several weeks earlier from Uncle Dick was now playing itself out in Cathy's life.

It was early that next afternoon that Cathleen said it was now time to for her to make that ride to the hospital.

Of course, she still hoped to return home. I looked at Cathy and said, "I do not want you to go. I'm worried you are not going to come back!" But with her strong, still believing voice, she reassured me, "It's okay. I'll come back. I'll be back"

I had to slide her back and forth across the slide board by the scruff of her pants. This while she held on to anything around her to get her eventually into the car. Then the same back out of the car again as she entered the emergency room doors. Cathleen Swenson was now back in the hospital for the last time. But she still was fighting for her life.

CHAPTER TWENTY-FIVE

The Last Room with a View

The intravenous fluids, the rest, and extra care did help. Cathleen would not be stopped. Not yet. This energetic organizer and planner was STILL calling and texting Linda from her latest hospital bed with more and more ideas about the church kitchen or the foods that were needed for the coffee hour that was coming up! Cathleen was still calling in on meetings with the church's Strategic Planning Committee while in her hospital room as well! She would not be silenced. Not yet. She could not and did not believe that she was near the end. She had to believe. We all do. She was not wired like that. She was wired to always be a fighter. We all should be. Now, this wise, fighting woman had overcome so many odds. She was just living and moving forward like she had always done in her life, overcoming obstacles and challenges, just like all those many times before, and she would NEVER willingly give up.

I knew she had been in a holding pattern for exactly

a year, starting around last year's Thanksgiving to this current Thanksgiving holiday coming in a few days. I quickly drove the three hours to Albany to see my family down in South Georgia. I visited with my sister, Caree, and her husband, Mike, and everyone and ate some turkey, made two sandwiches with fixings, and drove quickly back to Atlanta to the hospital so that Cathleen could enjoy a small Thanksgiving meal later that evening in her latest hospital room. The turkey and fixings were courtesy of my sister, Sally, and her husband, Buck, who had prepared it all that day.

And hey, Cathy STILL had a lot to be thankful for over all these long beautiful years, ever since the doctors from her youth had informed her parents that she would not live past the age of twenty-five years old. The doctors meant well. But they were wrong because they did not consider Cathleen's faith in herself and her belief in God. It is inspiring to see someone just hold on, since many of us do just that every day of our lives!

The doctors agreed that if she could get herself up and go home, well then, that would be all right since there was really not much they could do at this point except try to make her steady and comfortable. Cathy planned the next day to be discharged and had me bring her stuff. She was determined to get out of bed. All of this, of course, with my helping hands. But she was so exhausted from just doing that, that she started to black out in her wheelchair. "Let's go," she mumbled. "No, I don't want you passing out in the parking lot or worse," I cried. "Let's stay here and build back your strength back up. Let's do this right."

Cathleen Swenson was as determined as ever to go back to her life, and she tried, but she could not make it. Unfortunately, the odds that she had beaten so many, many times were slowly running out for our girl, who had outlived the odds countless times over the decades.

Well, this beautiful wife and strong mother had plenty of ups and downs in the hospital the last two weeks of her life. Just two days later, after trying to go home, Cathy's body went into cardiac arrest in the early morning hours. The doctors were able to bring her heart back to life after she had redlined for several minutes. The staff then induced her body and mind into a deep, dark coma, where she barely had a heartbeat. This procedure was done so that her body, her heart, and her brain could cool back down to see if she might recover from that massive heart attack.

My sister, Caree, her husband, Mike, and I, along with our son, Michael, all came to see her—Michael's dear, sweet, strong mother in this unconscious state. The latest wheelchair that she was using and living in was parked admirably and faithfully by the bed until the time that it would be summoned to ride her proudly again around the room, around the hospital, and maybe around the world again. We all can do anything we set our minds and our beliefs toward.

The medical staff now informed Michael and me that they saw little brain activity and that most people usually did not come back from this situation. The doctor said this proud paraplegic woman's chances were slim to none for recovery. So, Michael and I both said our goodbyes to Michael's dear mom while the breathing machine controlled and regulated her. However, the doctors said, "Come back Sunday afternoon, and we will try to bring your wife out of this coma, and see if she is still with us. We will see then what we have."

So, I came by again to check on my loving spouse the next day, and then went to church as usual on Sunday morning to be with my beloved worship community, where I served that day as usual as a staff musician. I really loved that church. And I prayed really hard and played and sang from my heart. Maybe they heard the emotion and care in my voice...hopefully, maybe. I was determined to hold on to some normalcy in my life, so I also planned to stay for just a few minutes after church for the congregational meeting, which plans out the future of the church and its many worthwhile missions. After several minutes, the plan was that I would rush off to the hospital for the inevitable, or hopefully... Only God knew.

Just as the after-church meeting started, I looked down at my phone and saw that there was an incoming call. It was from one of my personal contacts. The iPhone screen said that Cathy was calling. Was the nurse using Cathy's phone to give me an update? Was everything okay? "Hello," I said with a little courage and lots of trepidation.

"Hey, Sweetie…it's me, Cathy! Come see me at the hospital. I'm awake. I'm okay!"

"Woot woot!" I yelled and grinned while surrounded by my fellow church members.

"Share your news with us," said Ben, one of the many members there. I stumbled and bumbled to say that Cathy was alive and awake and it's Cathy! Everyone applauded and said, "Go…go and see her!"

I called Michael immediately at home and said, "Get ready to go see your mom at the hospital. Your mother is awake and you need to go see her with me!" Michael was thrilled but said his usual, "Okay, okay!" Always believe no matter what. Life is going to happen. But if you believe in good things, life and God can give you so much more.

CHAPTER TWENTY-SIX

The Visit and Its Aftermath

Around this world, cancer beats down and ends the physical lives of almost one million members of humanity every single month here on earth. Almost nine million persons living now on this planet are cancer survivors, meaning that they have been diagnosed with cancer and are still alive. Remember, the term *survivor* is a relative term, since we are all going to die physically someday—either today, or more likely in the near future or distant future. Again, distant being a relative term that is very open-ended. However, our spirit, our energy, which weighs about twenty grams per adult human being, goes back into the air and atmosphere upon physical death. Hence, the eternal debate *and* importance of life after death (i.e. eternal *spiritual* life, since the spirit does not go away completely but just changes form and shape…similar to water).

The point is that cancer beats and knocks down a lot of people in this world. About 1.3 percent of the world's population has had and is still alive while fighting cancer. And that number is growing. But that number jumps to about 5–6 percent of cancer obtainers and current survivors in the USA, China, and parts of Western Africa and western South America. And in Canada and Western Europe, it leaps to 7–8 percent of the population and is growing. However, in Russia, Japan, Turkey, and eastern Europe, the number boomerangs to 10–11 percent of the population being both affected by cancer and surviving for the time being.

Cancer is something that many, many, many people now have and have had in the past, and even more will be dealing with in the future. It could be increasing because it is in our genes and DNA now due to all of the extra carcinogens that have been created and pumped into the oceans, streams, landfills, and in our bodies. A lot of these carcinogens could have been created inadvertently as Neolithic farming humans (i.e. all of us living today) have gotten better and better at creating fertilizers, food chains, and modern farming efficiencies, such as genetically designed foods that grow better, multiply better, and thrive better in more climates that have literally given life to many people around the world who would be starving or not alive at all if it was not for the advancements in food production. (However, fair food distribution also needs to be revolutionized.) Science needs to learn how to clean up the carcinogens while maintaining a bountiful food harvest for all to partake in!

But cancer could be increasing because we are

diagnosing it better, and maybe medical science thought it was something different in the past. The reasons for cancer growing in the world and on this planet are probably a balanced mixture of all of the reasons above. But we always have hope. Look how far humanity and the earth's populations have grown since the beginning of the era known as the Middle Ages and then, after that, the Renaissance.

But Cathleen was no different than others on this planet who have had, still have, and will have the many different forms of cancer in the human body! Even though she had it five times in her life, hers is still a story of the triumph of the spirit to fight it off, to keep going no matter what, to live…REALLY LIVE until your physical body dies. The truth and narration here is that she survived and survived it well for almost fifty years, and YOU or your loved one or friend or community member can survive *and* thrive with it too! It is your choice. So just listen to Cathleen, she will tell you.

So to continue with her brave story and her fight to the end…

Mom was delighted when Michael and I arrived at her hospital room! She was childlike and ever smiling and asking questions over and again. "Tell me what happened to me, Sweetie. How long was I out? How long was I in a coma?" she asked. She was bright-eyed and her face was shining like the sun. There seemed to be light everywhere.

It was a great gift from God. It was like a rebirth. It was a shock and a great surprise to be with *her* again. As we spoke, she looked at the top of my head, which was often messed up or combed up, and said, "You got to do something about that hair! LOL." I was smiling but trying to defend myself, saying, "Um…I got up late this morning and did not have time to wash my hair." Yeah, right!

Then Mom looked at Michael's ostrich skin boots (that Michael certainly overpaid for) and said, "What's with those boots? They got holes all in them!" she giggled. She was so cute!

Then, she looked up, smiling at the top of my head, and said again, as if she had not said it before, "You gotta do something about that hair."

"I know. You already said that," I protested again with a defensive smile.

This fun and playfulness went on for the rest of the afternoon and for a few days. It was like Julie Andrews was now a working comedian, sharing her insights about life with sweetness and a devilish grin! Everyone in California was called and talked to her with laughter and some confusion. What was going on? Pete and Eva later told me that Cathy would start calling them every day until the end but would forget that she had even talked to them earlier! It was okay; they all were so glad that she was back with us!

Our dear friend Mindy came by for another nice, long

visit. Mindy and Cathy caught up more with each other, since they had not seen each other much; the pandemic had unsettled everything for over two years. Mindy loved hearing about the hair on the top of my head. She laughed so hard and said that's the way it usually looked to her!

About this time, Cathleen's wonderful cancer doctor came in to check on Cathy's progress. She had taken over Cathy's cancer care about two years earlier when Cathy's previous long-term cancer doctor moved to a new location. The doc seemed to notice that I was totally carefree and enjoying this special moment—maybe a little bit too much because we were not out of the woods yet, so she brought me back to earth. "Mr. Hairston, you know that after all of this celebrating we still have to get back to working on the stage four cancer that is going through her body. You know that, right? You know that she has not been able to take her cancer medication for some time due to all of these complications, right?" I knew all of these things, but sometimes you have to ignore the bad news for just a little while and enjoy the gift that God has put right in front of you. It is called simply being grateful and having gratitude for what we have been given by God, the Spirit. Then, after enjoying the blessing, you go back to work on the battle.

"Yes," I told her. "I know. Thank you." With that, I turned back to Cathy and Mindy and resumed this magical and blessed conversation with my wife, a conversation that I was so grateful to be having right now. A conversation and a moment that I did not think would happen a few days ago. Thank you, God! So, for a few quick wonderful days, Michael and I, and most everyone she loved, got to see her or talk and text with her again—what a surprise and what an inspiration!

But then again, just as quickly, it turned into goodbyes in person, or more likely on the phone. The doctors said this new state could not last, but it sure was worth it! Linda, Cathy's best friend from church, and her husband, Rob, whom I had known even before her when I was a mortgage broker, came up to Cathy's hospital room for a visit. There was some procedure going on, so I visited with them in the waiting room for a while. Linda was obviously worried about Cathy's deteriorating health, and the doctors had quickly started talking to Cathy about choosing hospice care. Cathleen and I had shared this with Linda, knowing that Cathy did not want to live in an unconscious and vegetative state.

In fact, the doctors had told Cathy that "she really was not supposed to be here"! Can you believe it? They found out after the fact that she had at home a written and signed DNR, Do Not Resuscitate, which they did not know about until after her first heart failure. They probably would not have brought her back and induced her in the coma if they had been aware of this. Cathy was amazed that they had put it in such stark terms but figured that they dealt with life and death issues all the time, so they were just doing their jobs. But thank God they did not know about it then, so that Cathy could have this extra time to say *goodbye* to a lot of people.

Soon, the procedure, whatever it was, was finished and Linda, with Rob, went down the hall to go see their Cathy, whom they had bonded with and toiled and planned and served with for almost five years. There was so much joy and smiling in the room. It was a great time together. But there was also a feeling of sadness and wariness that this was probably the last time.

In fact, the doctors had told me that another cardiac arrest and coma were coming—coming very soon— "unless you go ahead and make plans for hospice to deal with it. If not, Cathy is going to end up in an unconscious state in a rehab hospital with a breathing tube stuck through her neck to keep her going. She will not be aware of much, if anything," they said, "and she will not be listening much or talking at all. She will basically be back in another coma. And there will be little to no hope that she could ever bounce back from that kind of environment." Just like that, the doctors stopped explaining and said, "So, what do you want to do?" Well, there were not many choices.

However, this proud and gracious woman went back and forth on what she wanted to do because she had always been such a fighter. She had lived through and survived almost fifty surgeries, including fighting cancers, since she was fifteen years old. She knew that she had beaten the odds many times because she had never given up. On herself or on life! But this time it was different. There were so many issues now, and they had turned up the machines and were pumping her full of oxygen and the oxygen support tanks were turned up to the absolute maximum! Maybe it was time. She had fought the good fight. Sometimes in life you have to go with the flow and just give it to God.

And yet, she was still having a very hard time breathing and swallowing, so much so that the doctors were worried she might choke or aspirate.

Cathy texted me that morning that the doctors needed me to please come in once again extra early...that they really needed to talk with me and my wonderful partner again. When I got there to the room, the floor doctor, a male doctor, had already left. The other doctor was a woman—a physician's assistant who was probably put there by God to be the right person at the right time talking to Cathleen about this decision. A big decision—as big as they come in all our lives.

The PA laid it out for Cathy and me once again about the state that Cathy would end up in and that she would be stuck in a rehab hospital with little or no consciousness and a very low quality of life. Things that Cathleen Swenson had always fought very hard NOT to have!

Cathleen Hairston chose hospice that morning because the bright future and the normal life that this proud five-time cancer survivor and paraplegic had fought so long and hard for were already gone. Gone out the window. And with me next to her, Cathleen knew it. Cathy thought to herself that she was finally at peace and decided right then and there that she could soon let go.

That fifteen-year-old girl who had to start living most of her life using her trusty wheelchair had been living on borrowed time for so long. Cathy thought to herself, with her wheelchair still next to her, that she was now a sixty-one-year-old woman who had run out of currency; she had run out of time. That is something none of us can buy. We just live it and fight for it. And she could not buy or borrow any more moments. Oh, but what a life she'd had! "Don't feel sorry for me. I have had a great life!" she thought to herself. "NOTHING could take that from me."

So, hospice plans were quickly made for her sister Maureen to fly in from California on Monday and to try to have Cathleen somehow take an ambulance home to die in peace in her own home. If her being transported was not possible, then the high degree of oxygen saturation would still be dropped slowly in the hospital room until Cathy would be breathing on her own again...or not breathing at all. That was the question, but everyone knew the final answer.

Family and close friends in California and Georgia were called around noon to share the decision that the end was finally and sadly coming. Hospice had been arranged. Could it be true? She had fought so long and so gracefully! These calls out from the hospital included most everyone back home in California from where her life started, when she was still California dreaming and exploring where life might take her next! We all need to dream and believe! Even as she became paralyzed, Cathy had dreamed of traveling and flying to the four corners of the earth! And she had done that, and so much more! This life had taken her from a wonderful life and family in California to travels all around the world, in a wheelchair, to a very successful professional career and then unexpectantly to finding love with Cathy's very own family with me and our son, Michael. All of this, again, while being an early life cancer survivor and being limited and confined to an iron and rubber wheelchair. Earlier on, nobody would have ever believed that this girl with all the health problems would have been able to live this long and do this many things! She was blessed with this wonderfully full life and belief that would be her unusual life for over sixty years.

Her dad, Pete, later said that he had been waiting and bracing for a sad phone call for over forty years, ever since his baby girl first got sick. That last sad phone call of that day was saved, in fact, for her dad, Pete. For he had been Cathleen's "personal doctor" for over forty years and her first caregiver and always her coach, inspirer, and mentor with Mary right there, and later, dear Eva by his side. It was he who first held her hand and walked her through so many life and death situations. His young daughter that he so admired.

I did get Pete and Eva on the phone as the last planned

phone call this same afternoon, from the final hospital room of his tenacious daughter's life. A life where she had probably spent time in one hundred different hospital rooms. But thank God for that. All the hospitals and modern medicine and special care she had received kept her going until almost her sixty-second birthday. Instead of the predicted twenty-five.

This tenacious heroine told her dad of the hospice plan and that it was coming up soon. Cathleen said, "I love you, Dad," something that was very understood but not as often said. "I love you too, daughter." Pete responded strongly but softly… this big-hearted California dad. As I started to say goodbye to end the call, I looked up again at Cathy to see she was starting to pass right then and there. "Hey Pete? Hold on, Pete! Wait, Pete!" But Pete had already hung up the phone. Pete was gone. And soon, so was Cathy.

I stared intently back at her. "Are you okay, Cathy?" I said. "No, I'm not," Cathy answered softly. These were the last words to come out of her sweet mouth. But you know what, she was going to be okay because she had given everything, everything she had to a life that was well lived! And with that, Cathy closed her beautiful blue eyes, and she soon *flew* off to Eternity, where she continues to live with the Divine, as we each understand the Divine, the God, and the Pinnacle of the Universe. This is where we all will go one day. Are you ready?

CHAPTER TWENTY-SEVEN

Play Your Own Cards

Cathy could have given up on her life hundreds, even thousands, of times. But she didn't. Even with a wheelchair and cancer over and over. All those thoughts she could have had: why is this happening to me, does the world hate me, is it fair, does God love me, am I oppressed by this cancer, why have the doctors not fixed me, am I at an unfair disadvantage, am I discriminated against because of my wheelchair, will anyone accept me for who I am, can I accept myself for who I am?

Remember, it is up to you and you alone how you think and live your life with cancer or without cancer! With a wheelchair or with two good legs! Each of us can fight the good fight as long as we are ALIVE and live well and love well, no matter what obstacles or oppressions lay before us or what the world gives us or does not easily share. It is simply up to you! Just ask Cathleen.

Cathleen's spirit lives on with God and with those of us who loved her and know her and were inspired by her. She said many times, surprisingly, that the wheelchair was the best thing that had *ever* happened to her! "A wheelchair? What? Why is that?" Cathy thought and replied, "Because it made me who I am…God knows who or what I would have become if it wasn't for 'the Chair' and the obstacles. It grounded me and taught me humility and faith. It made me who I am."

Wow! If she can accept *that* about her life, should we not all be able to accept ourselves as we truly are and the situations that God and the Universe have placed in our own lives? Difficulties are a natural part of life that builds us, that strengthens us, and that makes us ultimately who we become! Many plants and trees simply cannot grow and thrive and reach their growth potential unless they are challenged to overcome and weather the environment they are growing within and around. Otherwise, they will die immediately. They certainly will not grow.

The Bible and many of the world's great religions and schools of thought have references to birds and flying in lots of magical and spiritual verses and writings. Whenever you see a cardinal (red bird), it just might be Cathy flying under the wing coming to say, "Hello," "I love you," or saying, "Fight On" and "Way to Go!" Cathy showed throughout her life that with a big heart anything is possible, even a normal prosperous life, even an extraordinary inspirational life. Even without two good legs or debilitating cancer, we ALL still can do anything we set our minds and spirits towards. But you have to put in the belief and the grace. Do yourself and the world around you a favor by blessing your

176

own life, the one that was given to you by the Divine, and simply agree to Play Your Own Cards! Play On. Here's to you being blessed!

Cathy STANDING next to horse with her other best friend, Linda. Around age thirteen to fourteen years old. Paralyzed WITH LIFE at age fifteen . . .

Postscript:

Cathleen Jo Swenson Hairston, sixty-one years of age, passed away peacefully with her loving and devoted husband, Charlie, by her side on December 10, 2022 at Piedmont Buckhead Hospital in Atlanta, Georgia. Wife to Charlie, mother to Michael, daughter and Cissy to her first family, and friend, cousin, colleague, and inspiration to countless others.

She leaves a lasting legacy of Love, Faith in One's Creator, and a willingness that says, I can do THIS... if I just BELIEVE!

About the Author

The author, Charlie Hairston, is also a singer/songwriter and guitarist whose love-inspired performances have been seen all over the southeast, including the music meccas of Memphis, TN; Macon, GA; and Dallas, TX, plus all across Georgia. He performs his jazzy original songs of faith and humanity, as well as cover songs, such as the Beatles, James Taylor, Jimmy Buffett, and Bob Marley. Charlie keeps sharing the love, the hope, and the joy of living from the Divine in all of his writings, music, and art. He lives in Atlanta, GA (USA) with his son and would love to hear more about your faith.

Great Lakes, Last trip . . . Cathy in Big Bear, Michigan to scatter her mom's ashes. October 2022.

Endnote

1 The accessibility standards set up by the Americans with Disabilities Act of 1989. By the way, thank you President Bush and Congress for passing this cutting-edge law and regulations. (I know many consider this a bad word.)

Milton Keynes UK
Ingram Content Group UK Ltd.
UKHW021136240524
442964UK00008B/33